❦ The Romance Factor

The Romance Factor

Alan Loy McGinnis

1817

Harper & Row, Publishers, San Francisco

Cambridge, Hagerstown, New York, Philadelphia
London, Mexico City, São Paulo, Sydney

First Harper & Row paperback edition published in 1983.

Library of Congress Cataloging in Publication Data

McGinnis, Alan Loy.
  THE ROMANCE FACTOR.

  1. Love.   2. Marriage.   I. Title.
HQ801.M47   1982   306.7   81-47838
ISBN 0-06-065361-2

   86 87 10 9 8

Contents

Author's Note

About once a month some patient at the psychiatric clinic where I work will, with a gesture of exasperation, say, "How can you listen to such depressing stories all day long? Don't you get disgusted with all these sick, messed-up people?"

I never know just how to answer, for those I counsel usually become cherished friends, and I'm uncomfortable to have them referred to—even by themselves—with disdain. I do not see them as "sick," but as fellow pilgrims who have many of the same struggles I have and who perhaps will gain some clarity as we look at their situations together. Not only do they honor me with their friendship, they continue to teach me about the human soul. And as we talk together about the inner recesses of their lives, I gain some insight into my own. It is to them that I wish to dedicate this volume.

For the sake of privacy, all case histories from my counseling practice are composites, with names, places, and details sufficiently scrambled to make them unidentifiable. The shapes of the people's lives, however, are true.

Many people helped in the preparation of *The Romance Factor*. Mr. Roy M. Carlisle of Harper & Row, a gifted editor, tried to make this a book with some logic to it. Mr. Mike Somdal went far beyond the call of a literary agent; he is a thoughtful critic and a cherished friend. The following persons kindly read the manuscript (sometimes in several incarnations) and offered their reactions: Dr. James Hagelganz, Cherry Henricks, Don Henricks, Dr. Taz Kinney, Tricia Kinney, Dr. Lee Kliewer, David Leek, Diane Mc-Ginnis, Dr. Walter Ray, Kathy Scroggie, Linda Somdal, Dagny Svensson, Mark Svensson, Dr. John Todd, and Wendell Will. Jarre-Beth Fees and Rena Inman were generous in their research assistance.

Acknowledgment is made to the following for permission to reprint materials:

Farm Journal, for extracts from "My Last Wonderful Days," by Hazel Andre, July 1956, © Dale E. Smith.

Glamour, for extracts from "Romance vs. Sex Appeal: The Battle Women Lost," by Harriet Van Horne, November 1961, © The Condé Nast Publications, Inc.

Atlantic Monthly, for extracts from "My Mother's Hands," by Robert Fontaine, March 1957, © The Atlantic Monthly Co.

In the relation of a man and a woman who love each other with passion and imagination and tenderness, there is something of inestimable value, to be ignorant of which is a great misfortune to any human being.

—BERTRAND RUSSELL

There is no surprise more magical than the surprise of being loved. It is the finger of God on a man's shoulder.

—MARGARET KENNEDY

Americans, who make more of marrying for love than any people, also break up more of their marriages. . . . But the figure reflects not so much failure of love as the determination of people not to live without it.

—MORTON HUNT

My chief occupation, despite appearances, has always been love. I have a romantic soul, and have always had trouble interesting it in something else.

—ALBERT CAMUS

In Defense of Romance

When my first marriage ended and the news began to leak out, I felt very foolish entering the pulpit each Sunday. If I could not hold my own family together, what possible counsel could I offer to others? Like most pastors, I was often called on to help couples with marital problems, and continuing that seemed the height of hypocrisy.

Late one night a parishioner called and needed to talk. I met him at the church office, and he began to tell how his marriage was on the rocks. He obviously did not know about my divorce.

"Wait a minute," I said. "There's something I've got to tell you about myself." I went on to explain the situation and said, "If you want the names of other counselors, I'll be glad to refer you to someone."

He reflected a moment, then replied, "No, I think I'd like to talk to you. My cardiologist had a heart attack last year too, but I still go to him."

To my astonishment, I found myself doing more counseling than ever, perhaps because victims of similar coronaries have something in common. Or perhaps because people want to hear from others who have learned some things the hard way.

The more I thought about my own failed love and the more troubled people I saw (counseling eventually became my full-time occupation), the more I realized that I still had everything to learn about romance and love. I needed to have answers to questions such as the following:

- Can old-fashioned romantic love work in this age of one-night stands and quick divorce?
- What *is* that initial rush of elation that causes two people to stay up all night talking? Is it a feeling? A force? A decision?
- Can you get the feeling back once you've fallen out of love?
- And why does romance die? Is it possible to hate someone you once loved? Or could it be that you never actually loved that person in the first place?

To answer these queries, I read hundreds of books and articles by experts in the field and talked to dozens of scholars—psychologists, sociologists, psychiatrists, social workers, and theologians. Not satisfied with their answers, I ransacked history books and biographies to study the great marriages and love affairs of the past.

After all the research, I'm still an incurable romantic. I've grown to have an increasing confidence that ecstatic love is a valid experience, that it is a category of emotion over which we have more control than we think, and that it is available to almost all who will commit themselves to the possibility of a great love.

We all know people who seem to be experts at love. People who know how to make love last and who have mastered the secrets of creating ecstasy in their lifelong relationships.

The purpose of this book is to pass on to you the secrets of these successful lovers. If you are in love, the application of these principles might help to keep you out of the divorce courts. Or, if you've already been burnt, and wonder, as I did, whether to try again, perhaps the happy ending to my story can give you hope.

There is another reason I still believe in romance. It is probably a more important reason than the research. After being alone for several years, I met and fell in love with a remarkable woman, and much of what I know about this subject I've learned by watching the way Diane artfully reaches out to me. After eight years of marriage, I'm still nuts about her.

How to Be a Better Lover

Look at those who are winners at the game of love. Are they simply lucky in their partners? Are they distinguished by education? Looks? Money? Usually not. Their success rather has to do with personality and with their skill at creating love.

These are not personality traits with which you are born, but they are qualities you can acquire. This is not to say that male-female relationships are simple, for in fact they are exceedingly complicated. Nor am I saying that the secrets of love are ever mastered easily. I am saying that there are common denominators in the great love stories of history, that these principles can be clearly identified, and that they can be learned.

Some people view romance as a great mystery, something that happens to them beyond their control, as if falling in love were like falling in a pond. But, as Erich Fromm says, the word *falling* in the phrase "falling in love" is a contradiction in terms. To "fall" in love denotes passivity, and love is the most active of occupations.[1]

You Can Generate Love

William Lederer, who writes extensively on love and marriage, says, "Love is not the cause of good relationships, it is the consequence of good relationships."[2] This is a very important point. Ordinarily, we think love must come first, and only then do we set about forming relationships. But Lederer says that it works the other way. An initial attraction may get things started, but *the quality of the relationship determines the emotions generated.*

A good example of the generation of love is the meeting of actor Robert Redford and Lola Van Wagenen. She was just out of high school, and he had returned from a lonely trip in Italy, where, he says, he had started drinking heavily and had begun to feel like "an old man."

"Lola's attitude," he says in retrospect, "was so fresh and responsive. I had so much to say to her that I started talking, sometimes all night long. She was genuinely interested in what I had to say, at a time when I really needed to talk. There were nights when we would walk ... down Hollywood Boulevard to Sunset, then up Sunset to the top of the hills, then over to the Hollywood Bowl and back to watch the dawn come up—and we'd still be talking. I had always said I'd never get married before I was thirty-five, but my instincts told me that this was a person I'd like to go through life with."

Later Redford found himself in New York, missing Lola. He called her from a pay phone, and said, "I have $32 in quarters. Let's decide whether we're going to get married or not."[3]

Lola knew how to fan initial interest into a flame. Instead of waiting for love to "happen," she created a relationship, and love was the natural result. They have been married since 1958.

So love is not a fiat from Cupid's bow, it is something you create. And when you have learned to create it, you have mastered one of the most important skills we can ever learn.

The Mystery and the Power of Love

Because romance is such a gossamer topic—what Henry Finck calls "a tissue of paradoxes"—some scholars take a rather dim view of it. One psychologist, having fed a mountain of data into her computer, emerged with the not-so-startling announcement that romance wears off after 18 to 36 months. Some scholars refer to our romantic obsessions as "pathological" and tell us that it was all an invention of the Middle Ages.[4]

But men and women fell in love at earlier times and earlier places than twelfth-century Europe. It was Helen's face that launched a thousand ships, and when Jacob worked seven years for Rachel's hand, the years "seemed to him but a few days, because of the love he had for her."[5] Passionate love has made the world go 'round for a long while.

Of course love is fleeting—the poets have been telling us that for thousands of years. But it is as perennial as the grass and it has been the source of too much beauty, produced too many sonatas, and inspired too many sculptures for us to contemplate life without it. Rather than dismissing passionate love because we do not understand it, we should set ourselves to study assiduously any emotion that is capable of inspiring a building like the Taj Mahal or an erotic poem like Solomon's:

> How fair and pleasant you are,
>   O loved one, delectable maiden!
> You are stately as a palm tree,
>   and your breasts are like its clusters.
> I will climb the palm tree
>   and lay hold of its branches.[6]

The Healing Power of Love

In the psychiatric clinic where I work, we deal with many collapsed lives. Occasionally depression has kept patients immobilized so long that I wonder how to begin. But sometimes, during the course of our work together, these patients find someone who loves them and whom they can love. To watch that happen can be very humbling, because love does them more good than all our pills and all our "therapeutic modalities" combined. I never tell single patients that they must get married to get well, but I do tell them that they must have some love, because there is, as Ashley Montagu says, "an awesome power in human love."

When the poet Robert Browning picked up two green-covered volumes of poems by a new writer, he was taken by their "strange and affluent rhythms." He wrote to the woman who had written them, "I do, as I say, love these books with all my heart—and I love you, too."[7]

He was thirty-six, robust and overflowing with energy. Elizabeth Barrett was forty, an invalid who had not left the upstairs of her father's house on Wimpole Street for over a year. But they fell in love. Tremulously, passionately, fully. As they saw each other more, she began to venture downstairs, and then into the garden, and finally, in September 1846, after weeks of plotting, they ran away to marry in St. Marylebone Church.

If such a love is pathological, then heaven be thanked for a disorder that could help an invalid walk and that could inspire the beauty of Mrs. Browning's love poems. One morning in Italy she slipped into Robert's hands a sheaf of papers that were later to be published as *Sonnets from the Portuguese*. One of these may be the best-known love poem ever written:

> How do I love thee? Let me count the ways.
> I love thee to the depth and breadth and height
> My soul can reach, when feeling out of sight
> For the ends of Being and ideal Grace.
> . . . I love thee with the breath,
> Smiles, tears, of all my life:—and if God choose,
> I shall but love thee better after death.[8]

When Love Grows Cold

But not every couple is as successful as the Brownings. In fact, one could make a case that love is one of the great disappointments, perhaps the greatest disappointment of our lives. Most of the 3.6 million Americans who will divorce this year once loved each other and will attest that romance is quite a slippery banana. They come through our offices every day—former idealists, one-time lovers, whose dreams have been dashed. Now they are angry, and although they are spending a lot of money for marriage counseling, they often take the entire hour to decimate their partners. Often our office is merely a stop on the way to the lawyer's office.

According to psychoanalyst Erich Fromm, "There is hardly any enterprise which is started with such tremen-

dous hopes and expectations and yet which fails as regularly as love."[9]

But love does not fail. Instead, it is people who fail. And
perhaps one reason we fail so frequently is that we enter
the wild, dangerous world of male-female relationships un-
aware and unprepared, urged on by a society that encourages everyone to pair off but that offers almost no instruc-
tion in the art of bonding. Yet at no point in life does our
ignorance and lack of preparation get us into so much trouble. The heartbreak, ruptured lives, and suicide with which
I deal are frequently due to ignorant handling of conflict
and to a neglect of rules that lovers have known for centuries.

So important are these rules that they should be taught in
every classroom in the country. You can live without
knowing the principles of calculus, but you cannot live
without learning how to relate to the opposite sex. Your
general happiness and even the success of your career will
depend in great part on your ability to create a happy
home.

Boredom: The Great Enemy of Love

For many couples who consider divorce, the problem is
not that they have grown to hate each other. They are simply bored with each other.

The ecstasy they once knew has evaporated, and not even
sex is fun anymore. An informal survey of sex therapists
conducted by the *New York Times* revealed that many couples are presenting themselves, not for treatment of outright
sexual dysfunction, such as impotence or inability to have
orgasms, but because they "just don't bother to make love
anymore." They are suffering from the sexual blahs.

Yet love need not die. A friend in her seventies astonished me by confiding that her relationship with her husband of forty-eight years was "still compellingly sexual." Occasional health problems cut down on the frequency of intercourse a little, she explained, "but the intensity is greater than ever. When we make love it creates a magnetic field that somehow draws us closer together." And another woman, married fifteen years, wrote,

We were completely in love when we married, and the honeymoon was something out of a storybook. The intensity faded, of course. After a year or so, we could tolerate brief separations, but Frank still phones me every day from the office just to see how I am, and I would still rather be with him than anyone else in the world. If I don't love him exactly the way I did those first few months and years, I don't love him any less. The love is different and still intense. I can't imagine it ever being less. We are different people now, but we have grown together in ways that have actually brought us closer than when we started.[10]

When Love Is Rekindled

The standard line, found in most textbooks on the family and dispensed by most mothers to their daughters, is that one cannot expect the torrid sex or the soaring emotions to continue. According to this point of view, one should be willing to settle down to a less-than-exciting relationship when other things become more important: the children, security, friends.

Although it may be true that the passionate, breathless stage does not last long (none of us could get anything else *done* if it did), the joys of love *can* be rekindled, and there are specific things one can do to become more lovable. In the next chapter, for instance, we will look at how little your good looks affect your ability to create ecstasy.

PART I

Four Suggestions on How to Ignite Romantic Love

Academic training in beauty is a sham. When we love a woman, we do not start measuring her legs.

—PICASSO

There is no such thing as an ugly woman—there are only the ones who do not know how to make themselves attractive.

—CHRISTIAN DIOR

Beauty, madam, pleases the eyes only, sweetness of disposition charms the soul.

—VOLTAIRE

Remember, all Tolstoy ever said to describe Anna Karenina was that she was beautiful and could see in the dark like a cat. Every man has a different idea of what's beautiful, and it's best to take the gesture, the shadow of the branch, and let the mind create the tree.

—WILLIAM FAULKNER

How to be Beautiful
Without Being Good-Looking

Many people suppose that they have difficulties in love because they've never found the right person. And so they spend an inordinate amount of time searching the globe for someone who can make them happy.

But the answer probably lies more in *becoming* the right person than in *finding* the right person. My wife and I have an extraordinarily good marriage. But Diane has good chemistry with lots of men and could probably make a happy marriage with several of our friends. Of course I'd like to think that none of them could create quite so exciting a life as I, with all my flair and finesse, give her, but I'm smart enough to see that her ability to be well married has mostly to do with who *she* is. Her nature is such that she could carry into any marriage an ability to love and be loved, to impart happiness, and to imbibe the joy of the moment.

Does it sound unromantic to dismiss the idea of star-crossed lovers and to think that my wife could be happy married to another man? I'm simply saying that success at love has more to do with personality than anything else. Good looks and luck don't hurt, of course, but we all know beautiful women who are always meeting "this wonderful man" but whose relationships are forever going sour. And we all know women of average looks who seem to have the ability to cause half the men in a room to fall in love with them. Such a woman has, as they said of Joan of Arc, "something about her."

When you meet such a woman and watch her success not only at attracting a man but in keeping him interested, you cannot dismiss it to chance.

Sex Appeal

For all our culture's absorption with sex appeal, little is actually known about why certain people are able to draw the opposite sex so easily, or why some couples are attracted to each other and not to someone else. What is it about a certain female body type that appeals to some men and not to others? And what is it about one odd-looking man that causes many women to be attracted to him rather than to better-looking ones? Such information has practical significance for the long-married person as well as for the single person: we all want to be attractive to the opposite sex.

Which brings us to the question "Just how important is physical appearance in the mating game?" Try reversing the roles and ask yourself, "How important is a man's (or a woman's) appearance in attracting me? And how important are looks in determining how I would enjoy living with him or her?" If you are like most people, your answer to the first question is "A lot" and, to the second, "Not very."

It would be hypocritical to say, as many of our mothers have said to us, "It's only what's on the inside that counts." For the initial contact, looks are a great boon. If you are a woman with a stunning appearance, you'll get to meet a lot of men who would not say hello otherwise. Which improves your odds.

However, the advantages are vastly overrated. As one beauty said, "Standing out in public has its disadvantages. You have to go through a lot of guys who are only interested in your body."

Because the great lovers are rarely great lookers, Principle Number One for igniting love is

> *Cultivate an inner beauty*

As corny and unsophisticated as it may sound, your ability to arouse passion in the opposite sex is determined by inner qualities, not outer shape.

I happened to have appointments one day with two women of about the same age. One had all the attributes of natural beauty: form, coloring, the right features, luxurious hair. But was she attractive? Nothing about her bespoke beauty. Her hair hung carelessly, her clothes hid her good features, and the way she slouched in the chair indicated a dislike for her own body.

Later, sitting in the same chair, was a woman who had much less with which to work. Her nose was considerably out of proportion, her feet were large. Yet I could not help being struck by the difference. This woman was absolutely fetching. She had sex appeal, and lots of it. The way she held herself, the way she had obviously given thought to how her clothes set off her beautiful features (and I, like most men, have never met a woman who did not have several beautiful features), and the overall impression of energy and femininity were smashing.

I know of no other way to describe the difference except to say that the latter woman had soul and the first did not. The language may sound strange when we are talking about sex appeal, but most men readers will know what I am talking about. Once in a while you meet a woman who has an inner magnetism, a power that emanates from her inner core. It affects the way she talks, the way she moves, the way she lets the wind blow in her hair, the way she holds herself, the way she looks at you.

The Perfect Body

If anything reveals the sexual neurosis of our time, it is the current fad of rating men and women. One man is "a 6," some girl is "about 7½," another is "a perfect 10." Presumably the number is assigned depending on hair, teeth, muscles, skin, and amount of fatty tissue in certain places. As if those features had much to do with erotic arousal. And as if one can only be attractive to the opposite sex for those years when the elements stay in exactly the same places. If that is so, Socrates is right: "Beauty is a short-lived reign."[11]

Women hit their sexual peak after they have begun to lose the form of their youth. Does that mean that sexual attractiveness begins to diminish? Nonsense. Some women cringe every time they see a man walking arm in arm with a woman who is obviously his lover and obviously twenty years his junior. They cringe because they are sure that sooner or later their husband is going to fall for some young schemer in the office pool. But such women do not realize what power they have over their men. Knowledge and experience, used properly, will be the match of any young innocent. Honoré Balzac was twenty-three when he was introduced to sexual passion by Laure de Berny, a forty-five-year-old grandmother. Their relationship lasted fifteen years. Maurice Goudeket was thirty-five when he fell in love with the French novelist Colette, who happened to be fifty-two. Goethe was twenty-six, Charlotte von Stein was thirty-three. Rousseau was twenty-one, and Madame de Warens was thirty-four. And Dr. Samuel Johnson was so devoted to his wife Tetty, an unattractive woman many years his senior, that long after her death he kept her wedding ring near him. Sarah Bernhardt was sixty-six when she began her liaison with Lou Tellegen, thirty-five years younger. When Tellegen wrote his autobiography, he called their time together "the most glorious four years of my life."

Plutarch said almost 2,000 years ago that "when the candles are out all women are fair.[12] And indeed great sex has almost nothing to do with the shape of a woman's breasts or the length of a man's penis. It is determined, as the song says, by what you do with what you've got. One man who had recently fallen in love with and married a woman not generally thought of as a beauty, exclaimed after the honeymoon, "Believe me, she's a beauty when she makes love. It's amazing what she becomes when she lets her hair down behind closed doors." If the sexual act is a wonderfully explosive act for you, if you notice carefully what your lover likes and give him or her lots of that, you can be assured that you will look very good to your lover the next morning.

Imprinting

"Those centerfold pictures in the men's magazines make me feel so inferior," a woman said to me. "If I exercised eight hours a day for life, I'd never have a body like that." Similar feelings of inadequacy are often expressed by men. When a man is afraid to ask a pretty woman out, he nearly always gives "my looks" as the reason. He does not think he is handsome enough. And of course, if a man feels bad about his body, he will indeed come across as unattractive.

Our reactions to certain stimuli are determined to a large extent by what Dr. John Money calls the "imprinting" of the culture.[13] And our culture, like no other in history, is trying to convince us that certain physical characteristics, such as large breasts, are sexy. But as Ernest Becker says, there is nothing per se about a large breast that has any more inherent stimulation than a small one. It is all in the eye of the beholder. Because we are eager for cues that give us a passport to sexual excitement, we respond to whatever configuration the culture has been touting lately.[14] In one era, it will be a full-bodied woman; in another, it will be the slender type. In one culture, earrings will help, and in another a ring in the nose is lovely. There is an infinite variety to beauty, for which we can be very grateful.

Art historian Kenneth Clark has examined the paintings and photographs of each culture's beautiful women. He says that there is little correlation between beauty and sex appeal: "Libido and sexual desire are aroused by some mixture of vitality, energy, and sensuality in a woman. Men can perfectly well see the beauty of a woman, and it will not fan any libido at all."[15]

Clark's reference to vitality and energy is much to the point. Although certain physical traits may attract initially, in the long run the ability to keep a mate interested is a matter of soul.

Beautiful People Can Make Lousy Lovers

In fact, one can make a case for physically perfect people being rather poor partners. The divorce rate is higher among startlingly good-looking people, partly because they have more opportunity to attract someone new when they get bored. But there's a more important reason why they fail in relationships: if you get a lot of attention because of the way you happen to be constructed, it is difficult to keep from becoming narcissistic and selfish. One woman was very emphatic in telling me that handsome men usually make the worst lovers. "They're usually self-absorbed," she said. "One man I dated for a while made 'working out' his chief occupation, and while undressing to get into bed with me, he'd actually look himself over in the mirror! I want a man who doesn't think about his body all the time, but instead is consumed with passion for me!"

A man may like having a beautiful wife to show off in public, but no man wants to be married to a woman who is forever retreating to restore her makeup, and whose primary concern is exhibiting herself to the best advantage. In other words, we like beauty, but we are turned off by exhibitionism.

Self-Confidence: The Ultimate Aphrodisiac

It is a strange phenomenon, but we have all seen it: people with large noses or glaring body defects—but who feel good about themselves—quickly convince us, without saying a word, that they are beautiful.

Grigori Rasputin, the libertine monk who lived during the reign of Nicholas II, had such power over people and was such a womanizer that people assumed he had in his pale blue eyes some hypnotic powers that women could not resist. He was fiercely ugly, but his self-confidence more than compensated for his looks.

Judith Viorst, a regular writer for *Redbook,* and a reigning expert on these matters, writes:

I recently met a woman who is fat—not plump, but fat—the kind of woman who should lose thirty pounds, the kind of woman who usually tends to hide in a loose black dress and hopes, at best, that her body won't be noticed. This woman, however, was wearing something flowered and quite low-cut, something that insisted on attention, and it struck me that she simply didn't see herself as "big as a house"—it struck me that she saw herself as . . . voluptuous.

The amazing thing is that by the end of the evening, I was seeing her as voluptuous too, for she held herself with such pride and such zest and such easy self-assurance that "fat" no longer correctly described her for me. I've watched other women carry off assorted imperfections because they were somehow convinced of their physical charms. And I've also watched women much older than I, free of the view that good looks are a function of youth, retain a composed belief in their attractiveness.[16]

I'm often asked to lecture to singles conferences and church meetings on how to get close to people. But during those seminars I devote considerable time to strategies for overcoming inferiority and improving self-esteem. For the better your self-image, the better your relationships. As Elaine Walster says in *A New Look at Love,* "Our ideas about ourselves—and the world—are contagious. When we are feeling good and are convinced that we are irresistible, we somehow manage to convince everyone else as well."[17]

Relaxing Makes You More Popular

If anything will make an evening with a new person go sour, it is anxiety and tenseness. A woman who primps hard before a date, and thus tightens herself up before the encounter, will be less than her genial best. A person who is relaxed and easygoing around the opposite sex will always be more attractive. George Harris, a reporter on psychological topics, says that, using the kind of statistical analysis that physicists use to determine the character of tiny particles, social psychologists have found that good looks, money, and personality all influence the romance market, but none of them ranks as high as the ability to be at ease.[18]

"Anxiety is love's greatest killer," wrote Anaïs Nin, the writer who was mistress to several of Europe's most famous intellectuals. "It makes others feel as you might when a drowning man holds on to you. You want to save him, but you know he will strangle you with his panic."[19]

Techniques Employed by Confident Lovers

When a person gains self-confidence, this inner beauty expresses itself in certain ways that are, in fact, physical.

1. *Confident lovers use their eyes to attract.* Watch any pair of lovers in a restaurant. There can be an awesome exchange of energy with the use of their eyes. All our talk about erogenous zones and the sex organs neglects one of the most powerful organs of all—the eyes. "You have ravished my heart with a glance of your eyes," the Song of Solomon cried thousands of years ago. And the people who follow you with their eyes, who look intently into your face, are still hard to resist. Studies show that if you hold another's gaze for only two seconds longer than normal, you have given a clear sign of interest.

Writer Marion Zola tells about a woman named Merry, who was visiting friends at their house on Fire Island. Walking barefoot along the bay, she watches the sun, hung against the pale sky. It is the quietest hour of the day. Everyone is inside preparing for the evening. In the distance, a man on a bicycle rides toward her. Suddenly, the bike is in front of her. She looks up, her eyes catching the direct gaze of a gray-haired man with a youthful, smooth face and slender body. He rides on with a boyish determination.

Merry walks on. Something about his face. Familiar. Almost Michelangelo's David. Only a second, but something had happened between them. She half turns her head. He is a block away by now, turning around to look at her. She is embarrassed. Twice more they look at each other with half-turned heads from growing distances. Merry is determined not to peek again. The gray-haired man turns his bike around. He pedals up next to her.

"May I have ten minutes of your life to watch the sun go down?" he asks.[20]

There is power in the eyes.

2. *Confident lovers turn up their energy level.* Anyone who has good results with the other sex knows how this approach works. A woman explained how she attracts men: "I'm not brazen about it, but if I want to get a man interested in me, I don't try to parade in front of him, or do any of the preening rituals that some people try. I just turn up the energy level. And I focus on him. I forget how I may be coming across to him. In fact, I stop thinking about myself altogether, and I concentrate all my attention on him. Maybe it shows in the way I'm looking at him or the way I'm talking—I don't know. All I know is that it works."

3. *Confident lovers touch freely.* Wonderful amounts of sexuality can be communicated with a light caress or a brush

against someone's hair. The tactile organs can, if used correctly, build an emotional crescendo. Sensuality is a matter
of attentiveness, of opening yourself to the marvelous sensations available to our bodies. It has nothing to do with
looks. Every man has a story about some dazzling beauty
who, once he touched her, turned out to be no more than
an icy statue. The famous St. Louis team of sex therapists,
William Masters and Virginia Johnson, warn against "the
fundamental error of believing that touch serves only as a
means to an end. In fact, it is a primary form of communication, a silent voice that avoids the pitfalls of words while
expressing the feelings of the moment."[21]

Here, as in the use of the eyes, the whole secret is in the
intensity of the exchange. And it is just this intensity that is
often missing between couples who have been together for
years. Touching your mate as if you were absent-mindedly
patting the dog is worse than not touching at all. Many
men complain that their wives are no longer sexy; but if
they resensitized their fingers and began to caress the way
they did while courting, they might turn their women into
veritable courtesans.

4. *Confident lovers seduce with talk.* I once knew a man who
was not good-looking by any standards. In fact, he had a
strange facial configuration that was a little repugnant. Yet
he was always surrounded by beautiful women. I once
asked him about it, and he explained, "If I can get a woman
to talk to me for just five or ten minutes, I know that I
stand a good chance of making a connection with her. So I
talk to lots of women. I know I can't depend on my looks
to do it, so I will risk quite a lot to get them to talk to me."
The mind is indeed the primary erogenous zone.

Skill at the witty line is not especially useful. Those who
have become successful at meeting attractive strangers say

that the single most important thing is to talk. Talk about anything. Do not try to think up some clever remark, but let the talk start as innocuously as most conversations do. Say "Hello, are you having a good time?" If it is someone in the elevator, you can say, "Hi, do you work in this building?"

Talk is even more important when you have been with your lover for a while. I hear every sort of marital complaint in my office. Some are ludicrous (like the woman who could not make love to the older man she had married because he insisted on doing so with the light on and his dentures stared at her from the bottom of the water glass on the nightstand). But far and away the biggest complaint, standing out in splendid isolation, is "We don't talk anymore."

I know that we family therapists have advocated communication until it has become a cliché, but couples who keep romance alive always talk a lot. Communication is to love what blood is to the body. Without it, marriages simply cannot live.

One wife who reports that her husband still romances her says, "It's the talk that does it. He seems to love to sit with a cup of coffee and just talk with me. Most wives don't have husbands like that—they're always buried in the sports page. But Hank tells me things. He expresses how he's feeling, and he wants to know what's going on inside me. That feels good. When he travels on business, he calls and tells me how much he's hating it and that he feels bad being away. If he feels *really* bad, he sends flowers. But I like it better when he calls. A five-minute conversation before we each go to bed means more to me than five dozen roses."

The Link Between Spirituality and Beauty

The Old Testament invites us to "look to the Lord and be radiant,"[22] and it has long been known that there is a correlation between spirituality and the magnetism you exert on those around you.

A man was describing a woman in her forties who is widely regarded in town as stunning. "But her high school photos," he remarked, "show her to be gawky and unappealing. Obviously she has developed a flair for grooming herself dramatically, but her blossoming comes from the fact that she is a warmhearted, generous person, a woman of honesty and intelligence, who has cultivated a rich relationship with God." St. Paul said 2,000 years ago that love, joy, peace, kindness, goodness, faithfulness—all the ingredients of beauty—are "fruits of the spirit."[23]

When James Bender was director of the Institute of Human Relations, he looked at the lives of a number of great actresses and discovered that none was naturally beautiful. Helen Hayes, Ruth Gordon, Katharine Cornell, Lynn Fontanne, and Barbra Streisand have magnetic and charming personalities, and some are clever in giving the illusion of beauty, but "not a single one was considered good-looking as a schoolgirl," says Bender. "All of them made up for it with inner qualities."[24]

And what of male good looks? Our most conspicuously handsome Presidents were men such as Warren G. Harding, James Buchanan, Franklin Pierce, and Chester A. Arthur. Not an especially effectual group. And who were the most unattractive Presidents? Men you perhaps know better: Andrew Jackson, Theodore Roosevelt, Abraham Lincoln. Their looks did not hold them back, for they developed an inner greatness.

When the editors of *Redbook* magazine published a questionnaire on female sexuality in October 1974, they had no idea what an overwhelmingly large response they would get. Over 100,000 married women (an unprecedented number of respondents for any sex survey) eagerly and honestly described how they felt about sex. One of the startling findings was that the more religious a woman described herself, the happier she was with her sex life and her marriage. This trend held for women of all ages—under twenty-five, twenty-five to thirty-five, over thirty-five: strongly religious women said they were happier than moderately religious women, who in turn were happier than nonreligious women. The most religious women were consistently more likely to describe their marriages and their sex lives as good, to be satisfied with the frequency of intercourse, to discuss sex freely with their husbands, and even to be more orgasmic.[25]

I have noticed that some of the most beautiful women in the world are to be found in churches. It should not be so surprising that Christians would enjoy sex more and feel better about their bodies, because the presence of God can effect wonderful changes. And ugly ducklings have a way of turning into swans when they realize that one can be beautiful without being good-looking.

Before closing this discussion of inner and outer beauty, I need to add a couple of disclaimers in order to make clear what I am *not* saying.

In the first place, I am not saying that because we value spiritual qualities we should take a negative view of the body. Quite to the contrary, the Bible teaches that our bodies are sacred ("the temple of God," in fact) and that they are to be enjoyed. At this moment your body is pumping blood through over 60,000 miles of blood vessels, receiving and projecting a myriad of signals, and all the while is available to give you a variety of pleasures. Most of us need to relax and take more pride in the fact that our bodies are wondrously made organisms.

Nor am I advocating that we neglect the care of our bodies. Some well-meaning Christians think that there is something "spiritual" about being slovenly or allowing themselves to get doughy around the waist. They are very mistaken. If you keep your machine finely tuned, your love life will be better both because the organism works better and because you will make your mate happier. The trouble with neglecting the body is that we are saying we do not care if our appearance displeases people who look at us everyday. It behooves us to do everything we can with diet, exercise, dress, and the help of professionals to be as attractive as possible. In this case, the motivation is not vanity or exhibitionism, so much as love.

The greater the man's soul, the deeper he loves.

—LEONARDO DA VINCI

It is hard growing up in this climate where sex . . . is OK but feeling is somehow indecent.

—MAY SARTON

Every time a resolve or fine glow of feeling evaporates without bearing fruit, it is worse than a chance lost; it works to hinder future emotions from taking the normal path of discharge.

—WILLIAM JAMES

My child, if you finally decide to let a man kiss you, put your whole heart and soul into it. No man likes to kiss a rock.

—LADY CHESTERFIELD

If we discovered that we had only five minutes left to say all we wanted to say, every telephone booth would be occupied by people calling other people to stammer that they loved them.

—CHRISTOPHER MORLEY

Building a Romantic Personality

"For the past eighty years I have started each day in the same manner," said cellist Pablo Casals at age ninety-three. "It is not a mechanical routine but something essential to my daily life. I go to the piano, and I play two preludes and fugues of Bach.... It is a sort of benediction on the house. But that is not its only meaning for me. It is also a rediscovery of the world of which I have the joy of being a part. It fills me with awareness of the wonder of life, with a feeling of the incredible marvel of being a human being. The music is never the same for me, never. Each day it is something new, fantastic, and unbelievable."[26]

Without knowing anything else about Casals, we could

surmise that he was a superb lover. Why? Because that daily gesture reveals a man deeply committed to the life of emotion. He is a man of feeling and passion, intent on discovering the wonders about him. And such a person, turning his attention to a woman, would be irresistible.

I talk to people who have never known a great love. "Everybody says I'll know it when it happens," a twenty-six-year-old woman declares, "but I've been waiting long enough." Such people sometimes need to expand their capacities for feeling deeply. They may be living such emotionally impoverished and cramped lives that they would not be ready for love if it came. Just as the swimmer stretches lung capacity by exercise, so we can stretch our hearts.

So Suggestion Number Two for getting started at love is

> *Expand your capacity for feeling*

In Defense of Sentiment

G. K. Chesterton once said that the meanest fear is the fear of sentimentality. Because some of us somewhere got the idea that to be mature is to be rational, we choke back our feelings and thereby we often miss out on the finest moments of our lives.

Why do we learn to squelch these emotions? One magazine writer tells how she witnessed a pathetic little scene on a country terrace:

On this sweet June evening, the younger members of the family, all in their teens, had foregathered for a nonalcoholic cocktail before going on to a dance. They were nice, conventional youngsters, tanned and scrubbed and terribly "adjusted." They talked of swimming and tennis and who had the fastest sports car.

Suddenly, far across the lawn, her white skirts almost ghostly in the gathering dusk, a lovely young girl appeared. Everything about her—eyes, hair, skin—seemed to glow. We older guests watched her progress with tender, if envious, eyes.

Clearly dazzled, a young boy . . . rose to greet this vision floating our way. "She walks in beauty, like the night," he quoted. Around him, like the shattering of a fine, rare glass, a burst of laughter! The boy blushed a dark red under his tan. "Or something corny like that," he mumbled.[27]

It was a painful moment for lovers of poetry. And for lovers of love. What sociologists call "the peer group" set this boy firmly on the road away from sentiment and romance.

Are Men Less Capable of a Grand Passion?

Somehow we males have been terribly misled on this matter. We have the mistaken notion that it is the cool emotionless hero, such as John Wayne or Clint Eastwood, who is most attractive to women. But the movie stars that women like best now are men like Michael Caine or Dustin Hoffman. And the thing they like best about them is their vulnerability. Perhaps women once looked for some Rock of Gibraltar on which they could lean, but they are now able to take care of themselves, thank you, and they're finding it hard to love a rock. Webster's Dictionary says that sentiment is "tender susceptibility." And if by that definition a man is sentimental, then under no circumstances should he try to hide it.

Contrary to folklore, the studies show that men are by nature more prone to fall in love than are women. When researchers at the University of Michigan talked to 250 young men and 429 young women, they found that nearly a quarter of the men had fallen seriously in love before the fourth date, but only 15 percent of the women. In fact, nearly half the women reported that even after they'd had twenty dates with the man they eventually loved, they had not yet decided.[28]

These findings do make a certain amount of sense. Traditionally, it is the man who calls, invites, pursues, proposes, and it is the woman who gets invited or proposed to; rarely is she able to select a man overtly. Thus, says Elaine Walster, "it is not surprising to find that the man feels free to plunge headlong after the woman he wants. Nor is it surprising that the woman is very cautious about openly displaying her feelings."[29] As one shrewd observer noted, "A man, when he marries, chooses a companion and perhaps a helpmate, but a woman chooses a companion and at the same time a standard of living. It is necessary for a woman to be mercenary."[30]

But whatever the reason, men experience at least as much if not more feeling in a love affair. In one survey, when asked, "How do you feel about being in love?" 38 percent of the men replied that it was the most important thing in life.[31] Walster cites abundant research showing that women are the last ones in and the first ones out of relationships, and men are "FILO"—first in, last out. Finally, there is solid evidence that it is men who cling the most tenaciously to an obviously stricken affair and who suffer most when it dies. So, once and for all, we men need to dispel the idea that it is unmasculine to feel deeply, to have a passionate love, or to show our hearts.

If we men were more free to reveal these feelings going on deep within us, it might prevent some wives from wandering. One woman said, "I am a wife with a solid marriage, a mother of three beautiful children, a career woman taking college courses at night—and having an affair for the past five years with the same man. I cannot really talk to my husband, but with my lover I am completely open and honest. My husband forgets my birthday, our anniversary, Mother's Day, in short, everything except Christmas. My lover is a sentimentalist who would remember Ground Hog Day if it meant something special to us."[32] This woman's husband is probably not unfeeling, but he has made the mistake of throttling his emotional expressions.

Reaching Back for the Child Within You

Becoming a more feeling person who can keep an old relationship alive is not all that difficult. One way is to reach back to our early years and recapture some of the abandoned emotionality of childhood. Jesus urged again and again that we become more like children. "No child is born with a really cold heart," wrote Lin Yutang. And, although we have learned to snuff out some of that warmth as we've grown to maturity, the embers are still there.

The best lovers forget decorum, and with the sort of exuberant joy with which a child flies a kite on a wild March day, they let passion loose in their relationships. Thomas Harris, author of *I'm OK—You're OK,* popularized the concept that each of us contains three people: a child, an adult, and a parent. In a lecture to mental health professionals, he once suggested that when a man and woman go into the bedroom to make love, they should leave the parent outside the door, and leave the adult there to keep him company. Then they can go in as two children to romp and play with abandon.

The passionate life is largely a matter of choice: deciding to shed the protective layers and practice the art of love. You need not wait until your romantic ideal comes along to begin, either. You can practice expanding your range of

feelings by going deeper with the relationships you presently have, by getting closer to your roommate or a friend.
The portfolio of emotions that makes one lovable to a
friend will be the same portfolio that makes one lovable to
the opposite sex.

Putting Emotions into Words

The ability to discuss feelings and to talk about your
emotions is common to all good lovers, because talk, not
sex, constitutes most of the intercourse between a man and
a woman.

A woman whom I've seen for several years, and who has
lost eighty pounds with the hope of becoming attractive to
men, has found that it isn't working. She is now quite pretty, but something within her that would normally attract
men is evidently shutting down. So I pressed to know what
she did when she meets a man she likes. "Well, I never *tell*
him I like him," she said. "That's the way I've always been.
When I like a guy, I go to any length necessary to hide it."

"Why on earth would you hide it?" I asked.

"Oh, partly because I'm afraid it would scare him if I
declared my love," she replied. Then she looked a little
embarrassed. "Also, I guess I'm scared, too. Scared of being
rejected."

Those two reasons explain why many people keep silent
about their affection. And so many love affairs never catch
fire: two people who are interested in each other are afraid
to expose themselves, and they wander away, neither ever
knowing that something electric was about to happen.

My friend is partly correct in her first point—men do
scare easily. But my observation is that they are scared by
questions like "When will I see you again?" but they are
charmed by questions like "Do you know it's been a long

time since I've met anyone I was so attracted to so fast?" The first is pressure. The second is warmth.

People who expose themselves by saying that they care will always build relationships. Which is not to say that it will happen *every* time you express admiration. But if you make it a habit to express positive regard for another whenever you feel it, you may be surprised at the amount of love coming back.

Hurting the Ones We Love the Most

The strangest thing in this regard is that we seem to have a penchant for expressing affection in reverse ratio to the length of time we've loved another. Except on special occasions, we rarely express direct love for those we cherish the most.

Not long ago I was preparing to catch a plane for Chicago. My son Alan, who was home from college and had offered to drive me to the airport, was helping me load the bags into the trunk. Scott, who is twelve, came by on his skateboard and said, "You're leaving, Dad?"

"Afraid so, Scott. Be back late tomorrow night."

He stopped his skateboard, put his arms around my waist, and with a big bear squeeze said, "I sure love you, Dad. And I'll miss you."

"I love you too, Scott," I said.

When we arrived at the airport, Alan said, "We're early, Dad. If you'll wait, I'll park and come in and buy you a cup of coffee." We visited until the plane was boarding. I rose and said, "Thanks for the ride and for the coffee, Alan," reaching out to shake hands. But he brushed my arm aside, put his big arms around me, and while we hugged, he said, "You know, Dad, *I* love you too."

Sitting on the plane to Chicago, I said to myself, "Mc-

Ginnis, what a dummy you are. What's wrong with you
that you know to give your twelve-year-old a hug and say,
'I love you,' then suppose that your twenty-three-year-old
wants only a handshake?" And there I was flying off to
give a speech on "How to Enrich the Quality of Your Family Life"!

There is magic in the words "I love you," and no matter
how well your loved ones know that you still love them,
they need to hear it again.

Judith Viorst, with tongue only partly in cheek, says,

Brevity may be the soul of wit, but not when someone's saying, "I love you." When someone's saying "I love you," he always ought to give a lot of details: Like Why does he love you?
And How much does he love you? And When and where did he
first begin to love you? Favorable comparisons with all the other
women he ever loved also are welcome, and even though he
insists it would take forever to count the ways, you wouldn't
want to discourage him from counting.[33]

Lovers who still have fire between them are in the habit
of discussing their relationship, talking about how their
love was born, reliving the times of intimacy, and sharing
with each other what they feel.

Sex is a good example. It should not be something that is
embarrassing for two married people to discuss, yet I'm baffled by the reluctance of couples to share what they're feeling during and after intercourse. Some lingering conversation could even help the pleasure linger. One beaming man
said to me, "You know what I like best of all about sex
with my wife? This may surprise you. It's the next morning at breakfast when she looks at me with a glimmer of
ecstasy still lingering in her eyes and says, 'Gosh that was
great last night, darling.' There's nothing in the world that
makes me happier than hearing those words."

Words are indeed conveyances of happiness, and we do well to cultivate the art of getting our feelings into language.

Lowering Your Expectations

In the early stages, a couple's passion is intensified by obstacles—parental opposition, forced separations, delays—and their dream is to marry so they can settle down and be "happy at last."

It is a dream doomed to disappointment, of course, because permanent joy simply does not exist in this life. Rather, God sends us happiness in small quantities, and then watches, I suspect, to see what we do with that before giving us more.

When I was younger, I had what might be called a plateau concept of happiness. I supposed that when I pulled myself up over one more ridge (like finishing a degree or getting some job), I would then step on to a plateau with endless vistas of pleasure. The consequence was that I was so turned to the future that I scarcely enjoyed the present.

Moreover, each achievement proved to be a hollow victory and never quite got me to the plateau. I recall vividly the long, hot commencement evening when I finally received a doctorate. As the ceremony dragged on, the sweat ran down into my shoes and I said, "This is supposed to be *it?*" Nothing had changed, actually, and life is still as full of frustrations with a doctor's degree as it was without.

Now that I'm older, my goals have become more modest, and I know that a day of complete happiness will probably never swim into my ken. Each twenty-four-hour-period has a mixture of joy and sadness, ecstasy and drudgery. On some days the mix will differ, but I intend to savor all the pleasure God sends, catching joy on the wing, to use Blake's image.

My goals for love have become more modest as well. I happen to be married to a marvelous woman, and we've been together enough years to know that there will be more passionate love on some days than on others. Feelings of romance usually come in trickles rather than in downpours, and once in a while there is a drought when it disappears for a time. But we do not panic, and we both have learned to cherish the minor ecstasies available on any given day. Like the quiet contentment of a Saturday lunch on our patio, when we linger in the sun to talk and she reaches across the table to squeeze my hand. Or an evening spent reading before the fireplace when, if we do not have a lot to say, it is enough simply to be together. "True contentment," said G. K. Chesterton, "is the power of getting out of any situation all that there is in it."

When I counsel couples, I tell them that romance and marriage have a lot to offer. Perhaps not as much as they thought at one time, but still a lot. And if they will value love, in whatever quantities it comes, and delight in it each day, they will discover that God can be very generous with joy.

Enjoying Your Mate While You Can

One way to savor love is to remind yourself that you do not have forever with your beloved. A few months before her death from cancer, Hazel Andre wrote an article entitled "My Last Wonderful Days." The piece was widely excerpted and has been reprinted all over the world. I quote at length from Andre, because her spirit is so much the spirit that makes ecstatic love possible:

Because my husband and I knew there was a chance I wouldn't be around, life became more precious. We crowded in extras, things we might otherwise have postponed: two . . . weeks of camping, hiking and fishing in the Grand Tetons. . . .

My mind and heart were watchful. I would catch a special meaning in a sentence. Like the statement at a women's meeting, that a homemaker's efforts should be measured in the moments of happiness that she gives her family. Something impelled me to slip away early from this meeting so that I could join my husband, who was going out to the farm. . . .

I have no regrets—my life has been rich and full; I have loved every minute of it. But if I were to live it over, I would take more time for the savoring of beauty—sunrises; opening crabapple blossoms; the patina of an old brass coffee pot; the delighted surprised look on a tiny girl's face as she pets a kitty for the first time. . . .

I would get closer to people faster. How much more Christian love there would be if we did not wait for death to release our reserves.

I would live each day as if it were my last one, as I am doing now.[34]

Enjoying the World Through Another's Eyes

One way we learn to open ourselves to the minor ecstasies is by watching people who are capable of such experiences, or by watching them occur in great literature. We can read novels for more than entertainment or enlightenment; they can resensitize our emotions, help us feel more acutely, and enable us to understand the people we love.

Psychologist Abraham Maslow, who studied thousands of people to determine their ability to have "peak experiences," found that it helps to be around "high-peakers." People who are more reactive, who get a profounder, fuller experience of life, can teach us how to do the same.[35]

I have learned to enjoy the world more by looking at it through my wife's eyes. She lets nothing laughable go by without laughing, nothing enjoyable without enjoying it. Last night, when the dishes were in the dishwasher, the two of us went for an evening walk. It was cool, and she immediately began to exclaim about how good it felt. "When I dream of summer coming," she said, as she tucked her hand in my arm, "this is the kind of evening I think of!"

By being with her at such moments of exultation, my own capacities for the minor joys are expanded. She knows how to tune in to whatever music is being played in the universe at any given time, and as I watch her doing that, it enables me to hear it also. "The world," says Chesterton, "will not starve for want of wonders, but only for want of wonder."

Learn to Savor the Moments

Three months ago, our son Scott brought home a crippled baby dove that had been thrown out of the nest, probably because he was sick. I discouraged Scott from trying to nurse still another waif, because every wild bird he and his mother had ever taken in soon died. But every day while Scott was at school Diane spent time tending the ungainly little dove. She placed his box on a heating pad, forced seeds down his gullet, and found the right vitamins to correct his weakened wings. And this time they succeeded. He has now feathered out and is healthy and beautiful.

When the dove was still very sick, Scott asked, "If the bird dies, Mom, will you cry?" She nodded. And he said, very seriously, "I thought you would. Because you have so much love in you."

Why do I digress in a chapter about romantic love to talk about my wife and the bird she nurses? Because the woman I love furnishes me with opportunities to expand my emotional capabilities. If you wish to learn to open yourself to joy, be around people who know how. And if possible fall in love with one.

An ecstasy is a thing that will not go into words; it feels like music.

—MARK TWAIN

You've been in love; you know what it's like. It's a sense of delight, not just in the person you love, but in all people, in yourself, in life. Suddenly you see beauty, excitement everywhere. You're not afraid to express your love; passionately, gently, in words, or in silence. And you feel strong, generous, fully alive.

—GEORGE WEINBERG

We cannot really love anybody with whom we never laugh.

—AGNES REPPLIER

Man can really live his truth, his deepest truth, but cannot speak it. It is for this reason that love becomes the ultimate human answer to the ultimate human question.

—ARCHIBALD MAC LEISH

She ran the gamut of emotions from A to B.

—DOROTHY PARKER

Creating the Conditions for Ecstasy

"It was the most exhilarating period of my life," Donna said, describing the week they fell in love. "We met at a party and were with different sets of friends but Dean's eyes kept searching out mine. It was more than looking—he seemed to take me into his eyes.

"We managed to leave together and then stayed up all night. It didn't take us long to learn that we're both pretty spiritual, so he said, 'Why don't we have communion together?' I think that's when I saw that he was different. The crazy guy charged off to a 7-Eleven, bought some grape soda and a huge oatmeal cookie, then we sat in the damp grass at the park and had Communion. We talked and talked and finally went out to breakfast. I felt that I'd learned more about him in one night than most guys had ever revealed to me. It was heady.

"Within two weeks we were married, and I'll never forget that month. Maybe it was because we both knew he was leaving for Vietnam, but neither of us seemed to need any sleep. During the day, we'd have fun doing ordinary things, like holding hands in the drugstore. If he had to go down to get gas in the car at night, I'd go with him. We took in lots of concerts that month. Sometimes we'd stroll down La Cienega looking in the art galleries, or drive down to the beach and listen to the surf.

"We'd make love once or twice a day; then during the night he would cuddle me while we slept and before we knew it our bodies were in motion again. It was a month of ecstasy. It was as if I'd never been in love before, and I've never been in love like that since."

Dean did not return from Vietnam. When I told the story to a cynical colleague, he said, "It's a good thing he didn't come home, because those two would have been in for one huge letdown." He puffed his pipe for a moment and went on condescendingly, "What's probably happened is that she has put a romantic glaze over those six weeks. It is a common tendency to put our martyrs on a pedestal."

My cynical colleague was saying that he didn't believe in ecstasy. Peak experiences are indeed a slippery topic, and there can be no doubt that emotional highs such as Dean and Donna experienced are temporary. However, psychologists have done some fascinating investigation of the phenomena of peak experiences and have dug up some data that just might help us in the art of igniting love or in restoring joy to an old love relationship. Suggestion Number Three is

Create the conditions for ecstasy

There is no universal agreement on the amount of control we have over ecstasy. Some believe that peak experiences come only as momentary visitations, and that we must, like C. S. Lewis, be "surprised by joy." Others, such as Abraham Maslow, hold that ecstatic experiences are much more common than previously thought and that, although we cannot summon such heightened awareness, we can create the settings that make them possible.

Research shows that there are several preconditions for ecstasy. In her excellent book *Ecstasy,* Marghanita Laski (who is not a psychologist at all, interestingly enough, but a novelist and literary critic) calls these preconditions "ecstatic triggers."[36] These circumstances are not to be confused with the experience itself, because they frequently occur without bringing about any heightened awareness. But they happen so often in conjunction with peak experiences that they are important to examine. The most common triggers are

- Art, especially music
- Natural scenery
- Play and rhythmic movement
- Religion
- Discovery of new knowledge
- Creative work
- Beauty
- Childbirth
- Sexual love

One cannot help being struck by the frequency with which most couples combine these experiences when they fall in love. They may have been largely unconscious of what they were doing, but note the way Dean and Donna packed so many of these triggers into their lives before he left for Vietnam. They took in concerts and galleries (art), spent time at parks and the beach (nature) played together and went dancing (rhythmic movement), had their own communion service in the park (religion), spent lots of time probing one another and revealing themselves (discovery of new knowledge), and, of course, made love a lot.

Most expert lovers manage instinctively to employ nearly every one of these inductors to heighten the experience. That is, the pleasure resides not merely in the enjoyment of the beloved; it is enhanced by a host of ecstatic agents.

The lesson that awaits us in all this data is quite simple: most of us know how to create ecstasy and bring pleasure to our mates. We went to considerable lengths to fuse all the elements when we won our lovers. But most lovers who have been together a few years have become dangerously negligent in planning for the continuation of such joy.

Love as Knowledge

Let's look at just two of these triggers and their importance in bringing romance to life: discovery of new knowledge, and sexual love.

Marghanita Laski deals with a whole group of ecstatic experiences that she calls "knowledge ecstasies."[37] These are moments of discovery and revelation. Most of us can look back to such moments of breaking through to some new knowledge. I shall never forget one day during my first summer in college. I was reading at a table on the abandoned third floor of our dormitory. Suddenly a passage from John Dewey that I'd read without comprehension the night before yielded its meaning. This time something clicked. Suddenly I was thinking thoughts I had never thought before, and my brain was connecting with Dewey's brain.

When people fall in love, they begin to make such discoveries of each other, as Dean and Donna did. Gradually they trust one another enough to open the boxes of the mind—some of which have never been opened to another person. Being invited to look in can be one of the most heady sensations available. As Erich Fromm says, part of the excitement of early love is the sudden collapse of walls—the bunkers of secrecy are broken down.[38] On a date, if one is successful in penetrating some wall—a wall erected for protection against others—it is tremendously flattering.

The experience of *being* known is equally ecstatic. Perhaps even more so. To have someone pressing to know you, someone who seems intensely interested in the things you are telling about yourself, is a powerful aphrodisiac. With such intense mutual penetration, it is small wonder that lovers stay up all night, talking and touching. We therapists also know the stimulation of having others reveal themselves, because our patients tell us things they've never revealed to anyone else. If a person has been coming to sessions for a long while and we have heard some of the same material often, it is tempting to let our minds wander. The way to avoid that is to ask ourselves, "What is different about this patient today? In what way has he or she changed since our last visit? What nuances can I notice that may, in turn, unlock more unexplored rooms?"

The assumption is that there are always new rooms to explore. Unfortunately, in a marriage it is easy to stop looking for these new rooms after a few years, to ignore the subtle changes, and to assume that there is no more to know. When two people have eaten several thousand meals

together and made love several hundred times, they naturally get lazy.

But if we pay attention long enough to notice, there are
always new things to discover about your lovers. Frequently a patient will say, "My husband tells people that he
knows me like a book, but he doesn't know me at all. I've
been coming here for only a few visits, and already you
know me better than he does." The sad thing about her
remark is that her husband could know her far better than I
ever could, if he set out to do so.

A minister urged his wife to attend a week-long conference in which she was to spend several hours a day opening
her life to a small group of people. When she came home,
she told her husband, "I met a man in my small group with
whom I talked all week. I don't want to hurt you, but I
must tell you that he and I became closer than I've ever
been to anyone in my life. We didn't have sex, but except
for that, I think he knows me far better than you do."

It was a shattering revelation to my friend, but he swal-
lowed his pride, and asked her to open herself to him in the
same way. He promised to try to be more attentive than
he'd ever been to anyone in his life. They talked for hundreds of hours over the next few months, and today those
two are very intimate.

Of course, it is often easier for people to reveal themselves to a therapist or to a stranger than to their mate, for
the stranger has no power to hurt them with the new information. Revealing and knowing each other's subterranean
depths is not always a simple feat for those who live together year in and year out. But it is worth whatever price we
must pay. We all have a universal longing to know and to
be known, the fulfillment of which is at the heart of ecstatic love.

Sex as a Stimulant for Romance

As might be expected, the sexual act is one of the most frequently cited triggers for ecstatic experience. There can be no doubt that sexual attraction accounts for a great deal of the intensity and joy we feel when we fall in love. One would expect, then, that all lovers who wanted to continue some ecstasy in their relationship would pay a great deal of attention to making their sex life rich and varied. However, when two people come to me because their marriage is in trouble, I almost invariably find that their sex life has fallen off.[39]

Therapists often comment to such a couple that poor sex is a symptom of some deeper problems. Solve those, it is assumed, and the sex will take care of itself. But sex is too important a part of the marital mix to assume that it is merely a symptom and that it will take care of itself. It is a basic building block for constructing and maintaining a happy marriage. A solid sexual relationship can keep a marriage together when lots of other things are shaky. And a seemingly smooth love relationship in which there is little sexual excitement can suddenly collapse.

Marabel Morgan, in her "Total Woman" classes, may advocate some rather outdated and manipulative techniques, but I like very much what she suggests about creating "supersex." Some readers guffaw at the suggestion that a wife meet her husband at the door some evening dressed in high heels and a babydoll pajama top, but I've never talked to a man who thought the idea was corny (as long as she got the kids out of the house first). And I've never met a man who objected to the "homework" assigned at the second session of Mrs. Morgan's classes: the women are to go home and make love to their husbands every night for a week.

One woman, on hearing that assignment, muttered audibly, "What do they think I am, a sex maniac?" Another woman, who tried it, said, "I attempted to follow the assignment this past week, but I just couldn't keep it up—I was only ready for sex six nights; Monday night I was just too tired." The teacher gave her a B, but her husband gave her an A!

And a Fort Lauderdale housewife told how she diligently prepared for love for seven straight nights, "whatever, whenever, and wherever," and it was her husband who cried uncle. "I don't know what's happened to you, honey," he said with a weak grin, "but I love it."[40]

We need leisurely, playful, whole-bodied lovemaking, and it is sad to see couples shut down sexually because they have been hurt in some other area. Sex should not be a weapon. I talked to a wife who was angry at her husband for a number of things. "How long since you've made love?" I asked.

"Several months."

"You don't have much sex drive now?"

"Oh, I do. In fact, I'd like to have sex with him, but I don't want him to get the idea that things are OK between us."

"So you just go without?"

"Yes, and masturbate a lot."

That's a sad story. Here are two people who are sexually needy, but are starving themselves out of pride or perhaps just to get back. And in the process they are further dismantling their already fragile relationship.

Fatigue and Marital Stress

As with the other triggers to ecstasy, the largest reason that people neglect sex as a vehicle for intimacy is a matter of time and priority. Husbands and wives see one another at the worst possible times of the day—a few minutes in the morning when they're pressured and trying to get on with their day, and in the evenings when they have no more to give and are irritable and exhausted. "There is nothing more certain to destroy a marriage," Dr. James Dobson contends, "than overcommitment and exhaustion. The breakneck pace squelches communication."[41]

A happy woman was describing the difference between her present marriage and the one that had ended a few years earlier. "My first marriage was virtually sexless," she said. "I don't mean that we seldom made love. In fact, we did it quite often. But he was so busy climbing the corporate ladder that he didn't give me half the attention he gave his worst clients. We acted as if we were sexless beings except for 15 minutes for two or three nights a week.

"Now there's lots of touching and sexy talk, and my husband sort of orchestrates the evening. He'll bring home some little romantic gift or a single rose he picked up at the florist.

"Sometimes on the couch he will kiss my neck or fondle my breasts, and it's not a prelude to going to the bedroom. It's just a sexual expression. Maybe we won't even make love that night, but I love to be treated sexually like that."

Her account ought to be a lesson for all of us men who know very well how to bring all the triggers for ecstasy to work at one time but who lately have given very little thought to orchestrating happiness. According to one study, it is not just men in our society who complain that they'd like more sex. The pollsters found that only 4 percent of married women thought the frequency of intercourse was too high, and 38 percent—almost four wives in ten—said they'd like to make love more often.[42]

Shared Ecstasy

To a large extent love is something you *do,* as well as something you *feel.* And if two people who once had happy times together stop planning to have fun, they quickly get into trouble.

Calvin and Toni were typical of many couples we marriage counselors see nowadays. They had been living together very happily for almost three years; then, when they married, everything went wrong and within eight months he had taken a lover. "I don't understand it!" Toni wailed. "We were so happy all that time in our little apartment, and then it was as if the marriage license put a jinx on us. The girlfriend he has now isn't even as pretty as I am."

As we pieced the story together, here was what happened. Calvin and Toni had met soon after his divorce, and at first they were carefree kids again. After years of painting and patching broken plaster in the houses Calvin had owned, he was free. When he and Toni set up housekeeping together, they didn't have anything to fix or anything to pay on. They'd even rented the appliances for their apartment. All he had to worry about was keeping his car washed and polished. So they went to the beach a lot, took fun trips on the weekends, attended the opera (about which they were both nuts), and had lots of time to cook together and make love.

After a while, they decided to put down some roots, so they bought a house, got married, and invested in an antique shop for Toni to run. Their dream quickly soured. The shop kept them busy every weekend, and it wasn't in the black yet. Calvin's list of repair projects for the house was getting longer instead of shorter. Suddenly they were fighting constantly. When they weren't fighting they were worrying about the antique shop.

I asked him about the new woman. "She doesn't mean that much to me," he said sadly. "It's just that when I go there for a few hours, I'm free of responsibilities and we can have fun together. The way it used to be with Toni." The problem, then, was not being married. They had simply dragged too much responsibility and drudgery into the marriage too soon. And they had forgotten to plan for some fun everyday.

Couples often say, "How in the world did we have all that time and money to eat out and have fun before we were married? Now we can't afford to go out for a hamburger." The answer to that one is simple: before you got married, you put a high priority on having fun. And some of us would be well advised to do a little more of that now.

I suggest that you catalog the things that could bring back romance for you. Some of the traditional symbols may carry meaning for you and your mate, but some may not. Rather than dancing at an exclusive restaurant, it may have been throwing Frisbees at the beach that was most romantic. The chances are that the fun things for you coincide with many of Laski's triggers and that they are often free. I talked to one wife who was disillusioned with her marriage because she and her husband had become so "serious" about life and hadn't had any real fun since the children had been born. Her husband claimed that he couldn't afford expensive trips. When I talked to them together, I asked them to write down the things they had enjoyed most when they were dating. They were

- Bike riding
- Cuddling up when it's raining
- Picnics
- Talking about happy memories
- Windowshopping at night
- Having a special dinner by candlelight

The little things count, all right, and often their only cost is a little planning and some expenditure of time.

The great truth is that women actually like men, and men can never believe it.

—ISABEL PATTERSON

I notice very much the way in which a man talks about women. I like a man who speaks with spontaneous affection and simplicity of either his mother or his wife. Some men cannot speak of either without a touch of facetiousness.

—ELIZABETH BOWEN

I kissed my first woman and smoked my first cigarette on the same day. I have never had time for tobacco since.

—ARTURO TOSCANINI

A married woman who likes her husband is much more attractive to men than one who doesn't. The reason is obvious. It's much easier to like a woman who confidently expects the best of you than one who has been soured by unpleasant experiences.... The married woman who instinctively likes men because she likes her husband is humanity's highest achievement.

—CHESTER T. CROWELL

The Battle of the Sexes

An attorney and his wife had been coming for counseling for several weeks, and I decided to try a private session with him. The chemistry between them was terrible, but I couldn't get a grip on just what was wrong. When the lawyer was alone and began to talk, the difficulty became quickly apparent.

"If you ever quote me on this, I'll deny it," he said, "but I've always believed that women were inferior, and my wife more than proves the point. If it weren't that I wanted a son so badly, I would never have married. In fact, when the kids are gone, I may leave too. I'd probably have to have some woman for sex, but I sure wouldn't get married again. If it's companionship I need, I'll take men anytime."

My training is to be patient with such people and to look

for underlying causes of such prejudice. But this time I couldn't contain my dismay.

"You poor guy," I said. "You're missing out on half the pleasure of life. Women just happen to be the finest idea God ever had!" In ensuing sessions, I managed to be less scolding, and my patient managed to summon more appreciation for the opposite sex. He took a second look at his wife, and when his attitude began to relax, she began to change.

If a man expects women to be inferior, or mean, or unaccepting, they probably will be. If he trusts them and expects them to like him, they probably will do that.

So Guideline Number Four is

> *Believe the best about the opposite sex*

Another man with whom I talked was not as straightforward as my attorney friend. He had been married twice and had been through numerous affairs, several of them with married women. At first he would be mushy in his rapture, telling her and everyone else that "this was the one." But then, as he got to know her, his enthusiasm would wane, and something always went wrong.

I asked for a description of his mother. She had been an unhappy and grim woman who had favored his half brother and treated my patient so badly that he'd left home at fifteen.

"Then maybe you don't like women?" I asked.

"Wrong, Doc," he said. "You couldn't be more off base. What do you think I am, gay or something? No, women really turn me on. I'd like to go to bed with half the women in the world. I *like* women."

I reminded him that I was not suggesting that he disliked

sex, but that he disliked women. I was asking if he could enjoy their company as well as their bodies. "Do you have close women friends? How do you like female business associates, or golf partners?" I asked.

At this line of questioning, he fell silent and finally said, "Maybe you're right. I'm really not very comfortable with them, and maybe some of my feelings are holdovers from my relationship with Mom."

Freud's theory of the Oedipus complex has taken the brunt of much banter from comics, but there is no doubt that he was right: most of us have, during childhood, something of a love affair with the parent of the opposite sex. Ordinarily that is normal and healthy. When a man has had a strong, warm bond with his mother and then distanced himself from her, he can become a good lover. I tell my teenage daughters that the best husband would be a man who really loves his mother. And lives 500 miles away.

But the love lives of some people get terribly impacted because of these primal relationships. In our work with patients, we counselors talk a great deal about parents—how to love them and how to get free of them at the same time.

Elvis and Oedipus

No better illustration of the complicated nature of these early experiences could be adduced than the tragic life of the King of Rock. Elvis Presley's relationships with women were all disasters, and sure enough, his mother, Gladys, was a doting, suffocating woman who seems to have spent most of her libido on her son. Albert Goldman, in his controversial and scathing biography, calls her a "Hillbilly Cassandra."[43] Until he was eleven years old, "Satnin" (Elvis's baby-talk name for his mother) slept in the same bed with him, and she still walked him to school in the ninth grade.

Small wonder, then, that he was never able to get loose from her apron strings sexually. He stroked and petted her until her death, and when the casket was opened at her funeral, he babbled childish words to her "sooties," their private name for her feet. Later, when he became more and more dependent on drugs, he could sometimes fall asleep only when Linda Thompson, his mistress, babbled at him in soothing baby talk.

It was a pattern throughout his connections with women: any who had ever born children were sexually repugnant. They obviously were no longer mistresses—they were mothers. When Elvis's wife Priscilla had his child, says Goldman, he stopped all sex with her and so neglected her that she finally left with a new lover.

Elvis's attempts at connecting with women were increasingly pathetic as his life disintegrated. He boasted that he had had "a thousand women," but his way of having them was increasingly unusual. He never went to them. They were recruited and brought to him. They had to be under eighteen years old, under 5 feet 3 inches tall, and under his spell. Some young women would cooperate by forming threesomes, wrestling in their underpants while the excited King, stoned and bloated with cheeseburgers, simply watched from his bed. At the end, he had periods of such heavy drug use that he could not get to the bathroom. His aides wrapped him in huge towels as a diaper to keep the bedclothes clean.

It is a sad story of a man who could have bought anything (he reportedly grossed $1 billion by age forty-two), yet could never sustain a normal relationship with a woman. The reasons are not simple, but at least part of the difficulty was tied to his early relationships. Freud did not invent the Oedipus story—Sophocles wrote the play in the fifth century B.C.—and we are not finished with it yet.

Living Down Your Past

If you have had sexual aberrations in your past, that does not mean that your relationships need to be harmed permanently. If your life with your parents was not altogether satisfactory, you need an accurate insight into your childhood in order to determine how you acquired some of your current disposition. Many times it is not necessary to seek out a professional counselor to go back over the formative experiences of the past. You simply need to open up the doors and relive the traumas. Keep in mind that you are not going back to blame anyone—your parents probably did the very best they could. Instead, you are pulling the buried emotions out of your unconscious, where they exert their silent pull on you, and bringing them to consciousness. The assumption in our field is that if the demons that afflict you can be faced and given names, you take away much of their power.

When you begin to make adjustments based on these new insights, you begin to look more realistically at people who remind you of your past. Instead of overglamorizing them or confusing them with negative images from bygone days, you can begin to like them (or dislike them) for what they are. We do not have to be imprisoned by the past—*that* is where Freud was wrong.

In clinics such as ours, we often talk to men who are expecting to fail with women. Like the proverbial dog, they expect to get kicked, and indeed it frequently happens. I urge such men to summon a little courage and begin spending time with female companions. Sometimes they can cultivate the friendship of an older, grandmotherly type, and with her safely explore the wonderful attributes in women. To get some small successes under their belts does wonders for the self-confidence of such men.

When Martin came in for his first visit, I waited while he squirmed and made tiny expeditions of small talk, only to retreat back to his uncomfortable silence. While we waited, I could not help being impressed by his good looks. He had broad shoulders and a ruddy complexion, and his eyes were as blue as Paul Newman's. Looking at him, I would have guessed that most of the women on his campus would have given anything to go out with him. So it was startling to hear him say, "This is embarrassing to admit to anyone, but I've never had a real girlfriend." He went on to talk about his introduction to sex in the back of a van: "It was only that one time, and I'd had a lot of beers. It sure wasn't all it had been cooked up to be. What I'm looking for is a whole lot more than that. I see these couples at school who hold hands and look as if they've got so much between them. I'm just too shy, I guess. I get so worried when I try to talk to a girl that I get an upset stomach. It's not worth it."

How could a man be so baffled by the process of love and feel so insecure in relating to women? It happens more often than some might think.

Shyness as an Asset

Philip Zimbardo, of Stanford University, has done studies revealing that 40 percent of American adults regard themselves as shy.[44] Ordinarily shyness does not immobilize people and keep them from relating to the opposite sex so completely as it did Martin, but many are as miserable as Martin. A shy man may admire some woman from afar, become obsessed with her beauty, and think about her most of his waking hours. It may be that she, in turn, has found him attractive and would love to know him, yet both will go on, never having an inkling that someone pined for them.

The happy news is that shyness can be an asset rather than a liability and that one can get over insecurities about love. In this man's case, he had never seen a good male-female relationship. The way a boy learns to love a woman is usually by watching his father love his mother, but at Martin's house, neither father nor mother was good at love. His father, whom he admired, passed on to his son his fear of women.

My colleagues and I set out to show Martin that his data was faulty and that he might find the women at school to be softer and less frightening than he expected. Group therapy can sometimes be very useful in such cases, because it provides a laboratory in human relationships. It is a safe setting where one can experiment, for instance, in learning how to relate to women. If one approach doesn't work, you scrap it and no harm has been done. Martin came to group therapy every week for over a year, and gradually he gained some experience in talking to women about his feelings. He found that they were not nearly so awesome and mysterious as he had thought.

Although Martin is still shy, he's had several wonderful friendships with girls. Last year, when he dropped by for a cup of coffee, he brought along a beautiful coed who couldn't keep her eyes off him.

How Feminism Can Ravage Relationships

Those of us doing marriage counseling twenty years ago were accustomed to husbands getting out of their marriages because they were angry and often because they were ready to trade in the old wife for a new wife. So we would be confronted with a desperate, pleading, tearful wife and an angry husband as they came in the door. Now often we see a reversed situation. It is the wife who is angry and who is making a middle-aged break for it. Ordinarily it is not because she has another man. But she is determined to make a change, even if she ends up alone in some apartment.

And I find it hard to argue with these women's grievances. Usually they have been married several years, and their husbands have been insensitive, condescending, and domineering. After that long, these women are sometimes so angry that they can't bear to have sex with their husbands, are repulsed by their little mannerisms, and are determined to be free regardless of the sacrifices.

Now it is the husband who has persuaded his mate to come in, and he is pleading. Awakened to the jeopardy in which he has placed their marriage, he is scurrying about, trying to correct the situation. The woman will sometimes say, "He's trying to change, but it's too late. I don't think I can ever have the feelings for him again that you ought to have for the person you're married to."

Such suspicion of the male has been fanned by the feminist movement into a veritable hatred of men. Perhaps it is necessary for the feminists—and I number myself as one— to overstate the case. Zealots seem to be the ones who get reforms started. However, the feminists who depict the male-female relationship as a battleground are doing none of us any favors. The novelist Marilyn French is a case in point. Her rage against the traditional role of male as predator is justified. But the alternative is not. My heart sinks when I hear someone say, "Forget men. Go off and live alone or with some sisters. You may need a man for sex, but don't expect any more than that from him."

Sisterhood is a fine thing, but for any of us to turn our backs on the richness, ambiguity, and mystery of the male-female connection is to deny ourselves much of the joy available in this vale of tears. We are *not* natural enemies. We were created male and female, equally made in the image of God. And, according to the tender description of the creation in Genesis, we are made for each other.

More is at stake here than equal pay and role reversal. We are, by declaring war on each other, undermining a foundational source of fulfillment: our ability to enjoy love. I hope women will not give up until the inequalities of our culture are corrected and will continue to point out sexist attitudes until we get them straightened out. But do not ask us to live without you. Neither of us will be at our best then.

In Betty Friedan's 1963 call to arms, *The Feminine Mystique,* she was raising important issues and they were ideas whose time had come. But now? Friedan says that the movement should enter a new phase and should not be so obstructionist about marriage and motherhood and nurturing. And what of her, personally? She has been divorced for years, living alone in Manhattan—but, she says, "I would love to have a good, committed relationship with a man."[45]

I guess I should not worry that women will write off all men because they have had some bad experiences. Nor should I worry that feminism will ever stamp out romance. Most of my feminist friends—some of them zealots—say that they have no aspirations for an isolated world of single-genderism. They do not intend to make themselves miserable in the name of revolution.

"Love is a great improvement on other forms of warfare," some anonymous sage concluded.

PART II

*How to Choose the
Right Partner*

The key to a rewarding, stable romance is knowing how to choose the right partner. Nothing can affect your happiness more than your choice of a lover or mate.

—MYRON BRENTON

It does not much signify whom one marries, as one is sure to find the next morning it is someone else.

—SAMUEL ROGERS

The most individual woman—and the most cynical woman— as soon as they fall in love, hasten to offer their whole lives to men who would have been glad for less.

—SUZANNE LILAR

I clothed him in the color of my longings.

—A PATIENT

Avoiding the Traps of Romantic Love

"How could I have possibly been in love with him?" a woman friend asked me. "After a year of marriage, I don't even *like* him!" Some genuine risks await us if we opt for grand passion, and among them is the trap into which my friend fell. What she thought was love led her into a relationship with a man who turned out to be a rat.

It may be, however, that love gets a great deal of blame that actually should be placed at the feet of our idealizations and our projections. The problem was not that we were led down the primrose path by the madness of love, but rather that we made a poor choice of a mate. And the culprit was that tricky tendency in us "to clothe another in the color of our longings." That is, we find ourselves alone and in a period of discontent and unhappiness; at such a time we are prime candidates for falling in love, and anyone handy can be the object of our projections. Unfortunately, that often gets us into lots of hot water.

Loving the Wrong Type

Some people seem to be lightning rods for lovers who are losers. Here are some observations on why we are attracted to the wrong people and what to do about it.

First, let's establish that love and compatibility are two very different things. Simply because we are profoundly attracted to people and have passionate feelings of love doesn't mean for a moment that we should *marry* them. Falling in love is easy. Some people can do it at the drop of a hat. But such people may have to fall in and out of love several times before they discover others with whom they could happily spend the rest of their lives.

There are also people with whom we are compatible, but whom we don't love. What we need is someone who is both.

Second, be cautious about qualities in your partner that look good at the moment but that are totally different from yours. It is very common for adolescents to fall in love with people who are very different from them. We may wonder, "What could those two possibly have in common?" Actually, they have very little in common, but the dynamic works this way: if you are unhappy with yourself (and most adolescents are to some degree), you tend unconsciously to suppose that someone with a different background and value system could make you happy. It is the lure of the exotic—"somewhere, over the rainbow" and all that. So the boy next door or the childhood friends who

share our history are quite unappealing. We cannot fantasize wonderful things about them. The stranger, on the other hand, can take on an unlimited number of our idealizations.

Dr. Don Tweedie, now a famous psychologist, tells about
some of the reasons he fell in love with his wife: she was a
free spirit, and her family was a carefree group that played
and laughed a great deal—all the things his family was not.
He came from a hard-working, no-nonsense background.
"It was wonderful," he says, "to spend the weekend at her
house and be around that bunch. We would play games and
laugh the whole weekend. She was just what I thought I
needed.

"But after we were married, I discovered that the very
qualities that attracted me initially were now driving me
nuts. I learned, for instance, that she was not only carefree
about playing games and having fun: she was also carefree
about the way she ran the house. Drawers were left open,
the water would be left running, lids would be off of jars."

Eventually, Dr. and Mrs. Tweedie worked out a fine
marriage, but only after separating for a year and rearrang-
ing their attitudes considerably.

What, then, is the answer to this compatibility question?
Should we marry people who are like ourselves, or people
who are quite different? The answer, as in most things, lies
somewhere near the middle. Certainly your mate should
have some interests that are different from yours—otherwise you are merely choosing a mirror. But unless you
have some interests in common, and some shared values,
there will be little on which to build. For a while after
Nina and George O'Neill's *Open Marriage* became a best-
seller, people told me that they wanted marriages in which
each person was free to go his or her own way. Unfortu-

nately, many discovered that if two people were always going their own way, there was no point in being married.

Third, distinguish between love and dependency. When people say they are looking for a strong person whom they can "look up to," and who will "take care of them," it is a sign of potential problems. If I love another merely for what the other can do for me, that is not love, it is dependency.

At our offices we see patients—most commonly young women—who try to take refuge under the auspices of an older more powerful lover. He may be a guru, a religious master, an experienced lover, who appears to have everything under control. The woman hopes that this leader's sure sense of self will rub off on her, but it never does.

Unfortunately, marrying someone who has the qualities we lack does not enable us to acquire those desired qualities ourselves. Marrying a total abstainer won't cure an alcoholic any more than marrying a musician will give perfect pitch to a tone-deaf person.

Fourth, watch for the fascination of evil itself. Consider, for instance, the Don Juan personality. Every woman has felt his allure. She knows he is a rogue, she sees that he treats women wonderfully at times and terribly at other times. But it is the very blackness about him that fascinates when she meets him, either in literature or in life.

Why would we ever gravitate to anyone who abuses us? Some of the answer lies in the enjoyment of pain, which is a deeper and darker topic than we are going to plumb here. But there is a reason that Samson and Delilah, Catherine and Heathcliff, Oedipus and Jocasta continue to live on in our literature. These stories correspond to an innate awareness deep within. We know that both good and evil are possible when a man and a woman come together. And whereas evil is always a little interesting, good can sometimes get quite boring.

Fifth, look for a happy person. The surest way in the world to doom a marriage is to play the missionary and marry some miserable person because you think you can bring him or her happiness. Beware of the person who seems to have no pleasure in life except when with you. It is rather heady to be such a rescuer, and it makes a man feel quite important if some troubled woman says she is able to forget her troubles only for the hours they are together. But happy marriages are usually made between happy people—those who were basically contented sorts before they married.

Sixth, beware of the excitement of a challenge. When we meet a person who is totally different from anyone we've ever known or loved, something about conquering this person from another world spurs us on. As I have said, much of the excitement of passionate love is the stimulation of breaking down barriers in another. The two of you meet, and the other naturally has his or her guard up. The question is whether you can break down the barrier. And until the last gate is opened, it is exciting. Herein lies the reason that some people lose interest in their partners as soon as the sex act is consummated. It was a contest all along, and now the challenge is gone.

Why the Bubble Bursts

Our mates do seem to lose their appeal, and the reasons are not all that complicated. For instance, there is the whole phenomenon of setting one's best foot forward when dating. We are not deliberately deceiving each other, but it is instinctive to sell ourselves. We look our best, we temporarily shelve some of our bad habits, and in general we do the things that make us look good. There's nothing reprehensible about that, but it *is* temporary.

On the other hand, you want your new love to look good, and if you're not living with a person, you can make him or her out to be whatever you want. If your ideal is a kind and gentle lover, you can fantasize your man into that as long as you have periods of separation when your mind can mash him back into that image. When a college girl writes home about a "wonderful guy" she's met who drives "this dreamy Volkswagen," or when a newly married man tells about his wife being a "genius" when she seems to have a rather ordinary mind, we know that these people are believing things because it feels good to believe them. But once they live together a while and see their mates under stress and fatigue, such idealizations will not stand up.

But there is another reason the bubble sometimes bursts: we are capable not only of positive projections when we meet someone new, but also of negative projections later. Let me illustrate with a rather common occurrence. A young man may find a new woman terribly fetching all during their dating months. But during the first month of marriage she may lose all her sex appeal for him. Why? Because once she is installed in the home, he begins to make all sorts of connections between her and his past. Suddenly she begins to seem very much like his mother. He had seen few such similarities during the previous months, but now he sees her in settings in which he experienced his mother—standing at the sink, taking a bath, digging in the garden. Or he may see a reaction in her that reminds him of his mother. The unconscious suddenly begins flashing "incest," and he finds himself strangely disinterested in taking her to bed.

Expecting Too Much from Romance

There is one more reason that the bubble bursts; it has to do with the idealization of romance itself. Sometimes the problem with romantic love is that we simply expect too much from it.

Someone occasionally says to me, "I can count on the fingers of one hand the good marriages I know. I'll never take the plunge until I find the right person, until the relationship is terrific." Such deliberation is wise, and such a high view of marriage is admirable from one standpoint. But it is dangerous from another. No matter how carefully such people choose their mates, they are almost certain to be disappointed when the marriage flattens out a little. And when such idealists find that their marriage is less than they had hoped, they tend to divorce prematurely.

Even though my work is largely with troubled couples, I know hundreds of fine marriages. Not ideal relationships, and not always passionately ecstatic, but good, nurturing relationships nevertheless. So when someone complains of the dearth of good marriages, I wonder if their definition is a little unrealistic.

We have been programmed by our culture, by the depiction of love on the screen, and by popular songs to think of love as the major solution to all our problems. It is the Holy Grail which, if recovered, will bring ultimate happiness.

This is a disastrous path, for we are expecting romance to give us something that only religion is designed to offer. When we begin to worship romantic love, it collapses under the weight.

Here is the paradox: romance can do wonderful things for us, but only if we do not expect it to do *too* much for us. When we accept it for the limited pleasure and happiness it offers, it can give us a great deal.

How to Keep from Falling in Love with Losers

If it is true that many marriages fail in the selection process, here are some simple guidelines to help you let your head rule your heart.

1. Choose carefully the setting in which you meet the opposite sex. A person you meet in a bar is likely to be a drinker. A person you meet in church is likely to be religious. This rule seems obvious but it's surprising to me that people do not plan more intelligently the places in which they look for mates.

2. Look for tell-tale signs, such as habitual undependability, womanizing, or difficulty telling the truth. We often miss these obvious tip-offs simply because we too badly want a person to be "the one."

3. The next suggestion is related to Number Two: avoid married people as a horse shies from a rattlesnake. If my practice is a sampling, the penchant for falling in love with someone married is more common among women. The reasons are not very mysterious: married men are safe. That is, it can be casual. She is not in as much danger of getting rejected, and she will not have to make any decision about committing herself.

Theoretically.

I have heard those reasons a hundred times from women who planned to keep it casual. And then suddenly they discover that they are in love. Most people agree that the life of "the other woman" is miserable, that her weekends are cruel, and that 98 percent of the time she comes out a loser.

4. Look for track records. You can tell a lot about people from where they've been. We should give the benefit of the

doubt when it comes to overcoming someone's past, like a troubled family or a nasty divorce. Yet it pays to look carefully at a person's past. Whether we like it or not, and regardless of our efforts to distance ourselves from our history, each of us is the accumulation of our memories. The leopard can change his spots, but it happens less often than some romantics want to believe.

Let's think again about a woman falling in love with a married man, and assume that he takes the improbable step of leaving his wife and marrying her. After a few years of marriage, the odds are very good that he will seek variety with a new mistress—just the way he found it with her. Many women sit in my office and say, "Why should I trust my husband? When he started having an affair with me, he was married to his first wife!"

The old bromide is that those who ignore history deserve to have it repeated on them. I do not wish tragedy on anyone, but misfortune does keep happening in the same ways and in the same places, and it behooves us to duck occasionally.

Love as a Decision

Some still believe that love is something for which you are fated by the stars and that when two people who were intended for each other lock eyes across a crowded room they will be irresistibly pulled together. To try to resist such allure, so the legend goes, would be trying to resist Fate, Destiny, Cupid, and the Divine Plan of God.

All of which is patent nonsense. As much as I believe in the joys of love, I do not subscribe to the idea that we must be at the mercy of passion. Quite to the contrary, I find that almost all of us choose when and with whom we are going to fall in love.

A doctor I know said, "I've fallen in love seven or eight times altogether. Looking back, I realize that in each case it was because I wanted to. One time when I was overcome with passion for this woman in our office building, I thought it was because she was so irresistible, but in retrospect I realize that at a not-very-unconscious level I was bored and looking for diversion. Any half-way attractive woman would have been fine."

The point is that we can see love as the beautiful and exciting thing it is yet can still exert a great deal of control over where our hearts are going to lead us. Falling in love is not something that happens by accident. We are to a large extent the masters of our destinies.

Let me be very clear that I'm not talking about mere sexual attraction. Most of us are turned on by lots of people in lots of situations. But if you're at all self-aware, your actions do not have to be at the mercy of your glands. You have the choice between nipping your emotions in the bud and fertilizing them.

A carpenter who had been badly burned by a divorce said to me, "This may sound a little unromantic, but I have a list. There are certain qualities I know I've got to have in the next woman I marry, and I'll be darned if I'm going to let myself fall in love with some woman who doesn't have at least the majority of those qualities. Sure, I'm sexually aroused by lots of women. I could fall in love with several of them, but I don't. On the other hand, when I meet the person who fits the list, watch how I tumble."

Not so stupid, this guy. And nothing antiromantic about that philosophy, either. He's simply accepting romance for the wonderful, if limited, thing it is, and is steering it to work for him rather than against him.

PART III

Four Ways to Build Intimacy
and Still Be Yourself

The entire sum of existence is the magic of being needed by just one person.

—VI PUTNAM

Almost no one is foolish enough to imagine that he automatically deserves great success in any field of activity; yet almost everyone believes that he automatically deserves success in marriage.

—SYDNEY J. HARRIS

And then I asked him with my eyes to ask again yes and then he asked me would I yes to say yes my mountain flower and first I put my arms around him yes and drew him down to me so he could feel my breasts all perfume yes and his heart was going like mad and yes I said yes I will, Yes.

—JAMES JOYCE

The supreme happiness of life is the conviction that we are loved; loved for ourselves, or rather, loved in spite of ourselves.

—VICTOR HUGO

Love and the Fulfillment of Your Needs

In this and the next several chapters, we will look at some of the reasons love can die. I can best begin by relating some things about the failure of my own first marriage.

It is difficult to describe how a fragile construct of dreams, shared needs, and accumulated memories can suddenly collapse. As I sat with my attorney in a large courtroom, waiting to be assigned a judge, I wondered what was going on inside my wife's mind as she sat far on the other side, with her lawyer. It was probably the worst day of her life too, and worlds removed from the day twenty years before when we had stood at a counter in the old County Records Building, just a block away from this courtroom—

two eager youngsters applying for their marriage license.

I wondered if she too had contemplated suicide? The humiliation, the sense of failure, the feeling of rejection. If two people feel rejected, what could have gone wrong? Novelist Kurt Vonnegut is right when he says that it's as if you've awakened after a terrible accident and find yourselves in separate ambulances, speeding to hospitals in opposite directions.

It has been more than a decade since that marriage ended. We are married to other people now, both of whom have given us what we could not seem to give each other. And, perhaps because of that earlier failure, we have forged good marriages the second time. And yet I still ponder the question "What went wrong?" No couple could have been more swept up in the romantic elan of the 1950s than that young couple applying for their marriage license twenty years earlier. Were we ill matched, married to the wrong people? Perhaps there were differences in taste and inclination, but we had more in common than some who stay well married. Did we lack training in religious verities? Surely not.

What, then, *did* happen? It is easier to be specific about my own failings—I was too selfish, too chauvinistic, too domineering, too much a hermit, too much a workaholic. Both of us could probably make such lists of regrets about our own conduct and grievances about the other's. There is a tendency to blame, to ridicule, but in the end it is well to leave complex situations complex.

For all the complexity, however, and all the issues about which I am still vague, I am aware that what happened was this: somehow two people who had been in love stopped meeting each other's needs. Perhaps they became too absorbed in other things, perhaps they each were too busy to watch closely the changes that were going on in the other. However it happened, their needs were shifting, and nobody seemed to be watching.

My work with troubled couples is obviously colored by all this, and I must be careful that I do not project my own past onto their experience. Yet I invariably talk to them about the mistakes my wife and I made, and offer some suggestions on preventing the death of love.

The first guideline is rudimentary:

> *Decide exactly what you need in the relationship*

I notice that most people who have long, satisfying love relationships have a clear-cut grasp of their needs and expect that a majority of those can be met in their marriages.

An Ideal Meeting of Needs

Lisa, for example, is happily married to a backhoe operator. She and Brian have been together for a lot of years, and one would think that any romantic gloss would have worn off. They're anything but starry-eyed kids anymore. Yet there is a strong loving bond between them. Lisa says, about the relationship, "Well, Brian may not be the best-looking man in the world, and he won't ever be president of his company, but if he ever died I'd be devastated. Not that I couldn't go back to work and take care of myself. I don't mean that. I mean that Brian seems to have made a study of me, and he knows how to make me happy.

"Music, for instance, is a very big part of my life and although he's not as appreciative of symphonies as I am, he doesn't seem to mind going at all. And when he brings home a new record he knows I'll like, he's happy. I guess because he sees how happy he's making me.

"Or take sex. I talk to so many women who complain that their husbands are clumsy lovers. Not Brian. He knows my body like a musician knows his violin, and he plays me for all I'm worth. He takes his time, he romances me, he plays with me, teases me. He lets me sometimes call the shots. I really can't imagine being any more fulfilled sexually.

"The same is true of other areas. There are certain things I want from life, and in my relationship with Brian I get most of them. Not all. But certainly more than I could ever imagine getting from anyone else."

Is Lisa's happiness due to the fact that she's married to a great guy? Yes, in part. But I know lots of women who are married to great guys and are still miserable. Why then is Lisa so happy? In part because she has unashamedly entered this marriage in order to have some of her needs met. (Which is not to say that she's in it *only* for what she can get, but that's another topic.) Lisa has a good understanding of her emotional makeup and has clearly communicated those needs to her husband.

Talking About Your Needs

In contrast to the exchange that Lisa and Brian have worked out, too many couples enter marriage with expectations for what the wedded state is going to provide, some of which are too rosy, some of which are on a collision course with their mates' expectations, and nearly all of which are unstated.

Joan, for instance, always expected to be a wife and mother. She calls herself a romantic to have such an old-fashioned view—a little cottage where she and the children would wait in the evening for her husband to come home from work. I don't think the fault was her romanticism so much as her assuming that Gordon shared the same goals. As it happened, ironically, he was something of a feminist. He was not at all sure he ever wanted children, and certainly did not want them yet. Instead, he urged his wife to move ahead in her career.

There was nothing wrong with Gordon's desire for a more unencumbered life or with Joan's dreams. Their fault was in never airing their assumptions until after each felt misunderstood and uncared for. Eventually there were so many rough spots that the bond would not hold. As I watched them part, I felt downhearted, for it was a relationship that could have been saved.

On Knowing What You Want

One reason we fail to tell our mates what we're looking for in them is that we do not always *know* what would make us happy.

I have spent thirty years and probably 25,000 hours listening to people talk about their problems. The longer I listen, the more I'm convinced that most of us have very little idea what makes us happy. For reasons that are largely murky, we have never taken a close look at our emotional makeup and its peculiar needs. We do not even remember what made us happy in the past, let alone know what would be pleasurable for the future.

Often I send patients home with a sheet of paper that has the heading "Twenty Things I Like to Do" and has blank space to fill in. It is their homework for the week. I tell them that they do not have to think of big things. They can list such simple events as settling into a tub of hot, sudsy water.

Many come back the next week with only six or seven items, a sign that they are out of contact with their deepest, most spontaneous selves. They are unhappy, and small wonder: they have not even noticed what brings them pleasure.

The remedy for this is rather simple. With some time and attention, and perhaps with some exploration of the unconscious, we guide patients to know themselves more deeply, to understand better what it is they are longing for, what they wish and dream for. Later, if the therapy has been successful, they should be able to write down, at one sitting, a hundred things they like to do.

So if you and your lover are going to work out a good exchange, the first step is to get to know your needs. The second is to articulate the sort of life you want. That is, talk to your mate about what would make you happy.

The Difference Between Discussing and Nagging

This principle of talking about your needs, like most good things, can be run into the ground. Then it becomes nagging. Some men spend so much time telling their wives what they need that their wives feel as if they can never do anything right.

How can you discuss needs and not nag? For starters, give reinforcement when he or she makes you happy. It will not help to complain constantly about how boring your life is, but it will do a world of good if you can tell your partner how happy certain things make you. It never hurts to reinforce positive behavior. "Rather than criticizing the things you dislike," declares psychiatrist and sex therapist Avodah K. Offit, "focus on what you prefer. For example, 'I like it when we listen to music before we make love,' will inevitably get better results than 'Can't you think of a better come-on than the same old dirty joke?' "[46]

Perhaps you need to sit down and explain to your mate some things about which you are unhappy. But be open and gentle about it. And make it clear that you're not blaming anyone. Say that you're dissatisfied and somewhat confused and you need to lay out some of your feelings.

The paradox here is that if you reveal some of your needs in such a nonthreatening way, it can make you more lovable than ever. There is nothing harder than trying to love someone who is self-contained. "He doesn't need me, a distraught wife said recently. He doesn't need *any*body. He could get along just fine on his own." I happened to know her husband, and I knew that in fact he would be lost without her. But he was failing to communicate that.

The Question of Selfishness

One reason we are embarrassed to communicate our needs is that it seems selfish. And selfish love, by most definitions, is a contradiction in terms. Once we enter the realm of romance, we supposedly should forget our biological instincts to seek pleasure and avoid pain and instead live purely for the happiness of our beloved.

This high-sounding advice can be traced largely to one Bishop Anders Nygren, who, in his classic theological treatise, *Agape and Eros,* drew a hierarchy of emotions in which agapic love is at the top and erotic love is at the bottom. Eros (which for Nygren includes sex but is more than sex) is I-love-you-because-I-need-you, and according to him it is always despicable. Agape, on the other hand, is the altruistic love that God has for us; it is always admirable.[47]

Authors such as Dwight Small can wax eloquent about the application of agapic love to marriage:

Agape is not born of a lover's need, nor does it have its source in the love object. Agape doesn't exist in order to get what it wants but empties itself to give what the other needs. Its motives rise wholly from within its own nature. Agape lives in order to die to self for the blessedness of caring for another, spending for another, spending itself for the sake of the beloved.[48]

My patients have heard hundreds of such sermons on agapic love (I have preached some of them myself), and they feel guilty that they lack such an ability to sacrifice their needs for their mates. For brief periods they are able to live altruistically and make sacrifices, but then they lapse into more normal self-interest. Moreover, they notice that their mates aren't all that self-sacrificing either.

These feelings are in large part unfounded. Some well-meaning theologians have overdrawn the distinction between agape and eros, and perhaps have even misconstrued the way God loves us.

Anyone who depicts God as a benevolent autocrat who loves us without needing to receive anything in return has not read either the Old or the New Testament closely. In the Bible, God is depicted as a feeling, responsive Father, whose heart is warmed when His children love Him. God does take the initiative, loving us when we are still sinners, but, long-suffering as that love is, He needs some response from us. If that is not forthcoming, He may turn His back on us. Bible scholars have discussed at length the cloudy topic of the unpardonable sin, and no one is sure of its exact nature, but whatever it is, it has to do with the person's consistent rejection of God, which He eventually finds repugnant. Even God requires some mutuality.

A saint such as Mother Teresa of Calcutta endures enormous sacrifices for starving and suffering people. Why? For the approval of God, primarily, but also I suspect, for the look of gratitude in the eyes of some child whose pain has been alleviated. She will never receive as much as she gives, of course, but their response is important. Their reciprocated love keeps her going. Conversely, even great saints do not continue acts of mercy indefinitely to those who curse at them. There are too many other suffering people who need help and who will say thank you.

The question before us is this: "Is it possible to love without requiring something in return?" My observation is that a certain amount of self-interest is always involved. And if that is true of God's love for us, it is certainly true of our love for God. We turn to him because we need him. There may be some admiration-love and some gratitude (which we call worship) included in the mix, especially as we realize later how much God has loved us all the while. Nevertheless, it is our restlessness, as Augustine said, that initially pushes us Godward. "We are all God-seekers because we need to be fulfilled by him," according to the modern theologian Lewis Smedes.[49] If our restless hearts prompt us to look upward, then there is nothing ignoble about a similar restlessness that prompts the union between a man and a woman.

I wish to be very clear about this point: I am not advocating selfishness. I am describing love as a combination of appreciation for the beloved and a longing for personal fulfillment.

A Word in Defense of Eros

I now want to lodge a word in defense of eros, which has had rough handling in many circles. The reason for such treatment, as noted, is that eros is "needlove"—it does not flow from the unselfish goodness of one's being. C. S. Lewis is especially unhappy with eros. In his excoriating attack on Venus in *The Four Loves,* he damns romantic love in general and erotic love in particular,[50] a view that I choose to attribute to the fact that he married late in life. Had he settled into the marriage bed sooner, we might have been spared this harshness.

Most Christian literature denigrates simple sexual passion as being hedonistic and encourages us, as it should, to make sex symbolic of something greater. We must concede that there is a large degree of self-gratification in erotic love, but is sexual desire, in and of itself, a bad thing? Consider eros at its most elemental level: the simple desire to copulate. This desire is not only at the core of our being—it is also a God-given instinct. And since God created it as an intensely pleasurable experience, He presumably expected us to enjoy ourselves in the act. How then can such desire, in and of itself, be sinful?

Consider a plant foreman who comes home late at night. He is very tired, and when he is tired he gets a little obsessive about sex. So he is already thinking about making love as he drives into the garage. He knows that his wife will be in bed reading, probably naked under the covers. When he crawls under and feels her curves, he is immediately aroused. At the moment he is primarily concerned about his own needs. He wants her body. It is that simple.

Is such raw animal passion sinful? Some thinkers suppose so. He is, in one marriage counselor's words, "seeking self-gratification by means of another," and with such a definition the counselor supposes that he is pointing out how evil such erotic desire is.

But most women do not see it as evil. In fact I cannot recall a woman ever telling me that she was sorry to have a body that turns men on. Sometimes they say that it creates problems, and they often tell me that their husbands should take more time. But raw animal passion? They like it.

Let us agree, then, that pleasure by means of the one we love is inherently good, not bad. It is only when we take

our pleasure at the *expense* of others that eros becomes ma-
nipulation. That is a topic of some importance to which we
must address ourselves later.

The point at which Bishop Nygren took the wrong turn
(and a critical misturn it was) is at Christ's second great
commandment. Our Lord did not urge us to love our
neighbor (and our husbands and wives) instead of ourselves,
but *as* ourselves.[51] Yet Nygren can say,

Christianity does not recognize self-love as Christian. It recog-
nizes love to God and love to one's neighbor, but self-love is the
great enemy which must be overcome. Self-love separates man
from God; it blocks the channels of self-spending and self-offer-
ing, both toward God and toward man.[52]

As with most heretics, Nygren has a modicum of truth
mixed in with his error, but he misses the point of what is
perhaps the most profound psychological remark ever
made.

This discussion leads us to a topic against which we have
bumped several times in these discussions and which we
must now examine in detail: the relationship between identity and intimacy.

What a man thinks of himself . . . determines his fate.

—HENRY DAVID THOREAU

Only those who *can* live alone are able to live well with another.

—TAZ W. KINNEY

The marriage of the 1980s is likely to be more a joining of equals, and neither of the partners will expect the other to fulfill all of his or her needs. They commit to each other because they find consistent pleasure and emotional sustenance in it, and not because they are afraid to be alone.

—JIM SANDERSON

We would much rather blame someone or something for making us feel unhappy than take the steps to make ourselves feel better.

—MILDRED NEWMAN AND BERNARD BERKOWITZ

Self-confidence is the first requisite to great undertakings.

—SAMUEL JOHNSON

Independence as a Virtue

Many people think that self-depreciation is a fine, old-fashioned virtue, and that it makes for good relationships. But the good lovers are not the Caspar Milquetoasts of the world. Rather they are the self-starting and self-assured people who have many sources of pleasure, are wide-eyed to the wonders of the world, and are glad to share that life with you.

I talked to just such a woman recently, a handsome widow whose marriage had been a rich, equal partnership. She has a career now, she does not need a man for financial reasons, and she has plenty of friends. "Yet," she says, "I hope the Lord sends a man into my life. It's not that I'm desperate or that I need a man to lean on. I'm as good at fixing a leaky pipe or choosing a repairman for the car as anyone. I've got a full life, but I'd love to have someone to share it with. I'd like a strong man that I could come together with in the evening. During the day when I have to hassle with clients it would be nice to know there's someone with whom I'll talk tonight who cares how my day went. And I want someone to do things for and care for in the same way."

With such a view of love, she should be able to connect very gracefully indeed with some man, and he will be a fortunate guy. For those are the best prospects for a great love relationship: people who *can* live alone, who know how to be self-sufficient, who are not dependent on others for their very lifeblood, but whose happiness would be enhanced if they could share their days.

So Guideline Number Two for avoiding the death of love is this:

> *Cultivate independence*

One of the most colorful figures in the history of psychoanalysis is Erik Erikson. He has shuttled back and forth between Europe and America, between art and psychology; he has never bothered to get a college degree, yet is widely regarded as the most erudite and seminal thinker on the topic of identity formation. According to Erikson's model, one must acquire identity before intimacy is possible. It is not until adolescence, when you finally push away from your parents and achieve a reasonably consolidated identity of your own, that you can "face the fear of ego loss in situations which call for self-abandon."[53]

But Erikson was far from the first to observe that fundamental requirement for intimacy. When Christ said that we are to love our neighbors as ourselves, the same principle was operative. He was saying that we can only love others to the extent that we are happy with ourselves.

Developing Your Individuality

The corollary of Christ's great commandment is that to love well we must be developing, expanding persons who are regularly redefining ourselves. Since God created each of us different—our personalities as unique as our fingerprints—He meant us to develop that uniqueness, to become the distinctive persons we were meant to be. When Nicholas Johnson was head of the Federal Communications Commission, he wrote in the *Saturday Review* some excellent suggestions for identity formation:

You need to discover who *you* are; what feels right and best for you. You not only need to walk to the sound of a different drummer, you need to be that different drummer. You need to write your own music. You need to look inside yourself and see what is there. I think some time in the woods is useful for this purpose. But camping may not make sense for you, for a variety of understandable reasons. That's fine. . . . The point is to find your own soul and kick it, poke it with a stick, see if it's still alive, and then watch which way it moves.[54]

Living by Principles

I am not arguing that you should become a recluse or an eccentric (although a happy eccentric is probably easier to love than someone overly anxious to please). A certain amount of compromise and pliability is necessary for any close relationship to endure. But it is possible to be too flexible.

In novels a character may say, "I love that woman so much that I'd kill for her. I'd lie, cheat, do anything." Such blind allegiance sounds terribly dashing and romantic, but upon reflection, it is a sign that such a person has no essential self. We want lovers who have some center, some line beyond which they will not go. Exactly what the line demarking this essential self is, we cannot always say. It differs from person to person, and most of us are in flux. But in certain situations we discover loyalties and belief systems that are firm and nonnegotiable.

William Kilpatrick, in his able book *Identity & Intimacy,* gives the life of Thomas More as a paradigm for such self-definition. When More openly disapproved of King Henry VIII's marriage to Anne Boleyn, he knew he was jeopardizing his life. More was not some vain idealist. On the contrary, he was a skilled lawyer and knew the art of compromise exceedingly well. But to approve of the marriage required him to swear to something he considered untrue, something that constituted a denial of God's revelation.[55]

In Robert Bolt's play *A Man for All Seasons,* More's family visits him in jail, desperately pleading that he recant. To his daughter he says,

When a man takes an oath, Meg, he's holding his own self in his hands. Like water. [He cups his hands.] And if he opens his fingers *then*—he needn't hope to find himself again.[56]

The rest of the story is well known. More stood trial, and was executed. In Bolt's preface to the play, he makes an eloquent statement about Thomas More and the boundaries of one's soul:

He knew where he began and left off, what area of himself he could yield to the encroachments of his enemies, and what to the encroachments of those he loved. It was a substantial area in both cases, for he had a proper sense of fear and was a busy lover. . . . But at length he was asked to retreat from that final area where he located his self. And there this supple, humorous, unassuming, and sophisticated person . . . was overtaken by an absolutely primitive rigor, and could no more be budged than a cliff.[57]

One should *not* sacrifice everything for family. I want a lover who, like Thomas More, has a line beyond which she will not go. I do not want a wife who will do "anything" for me, because I'm not always entirely stable, and at those times I want her allegiance to be to higher truths than my own fickle perceptions of reality. It is what brings me back to my senses.

"Dwindling" into a Wife

Not only must one enter a love relationship with good identity formation; it is also essential to *maintain* one's individuality. This has been easier for men than for women, given our society's expectation that a woman is built to be dependent. Although she may have been functioning as an independent, self-starting person before the marriage— while in college, for instance—she is, in William Congreve's phrase, often expected to "dwindle" into a wife.

For all the traditionalists' talk about the glories of being a homemaker, wife, and mother (and there are indeed many aspects of glory in these roles), we see all too many female patients who have dwindled. Alice Rossi observes that many women lose ground in personal development and self-esteem during the early and middle years of adulthood, whereas men are gaining ground during the same years as they compete and achieve in the working world.[58] We see women who are quite able to take care of themselves before marriage but who have become helpless after fifteen or twenty years of marriage. Psychiatrist Genevieve Knupfer describes a woman who had managed several foreign tours before marriage: when widowed at the age of fifty-five, she had to ask friends how to get a passport.[59]

It would be foolish to suggest that every woman must work to be fulfilled and growing, but every woman should have some passionate interests. And in pursuing some of those interests, she should get out of the home regularly.

The Dangers of Stagnation

In other words, we all owe our mates as well as ourselves the promise that we will not stagnate. We hope that our partners will not wake up in twenty years and find that we have not changed except to acquire wrinkles. Benjamin Jowett, the great British preacher, once remarked, "I hate to meet a man whom I have known ten years ago and find that he is at precisely the same point, neither moderated nor quickened nor experienced but simply stiffened."[60] Identity and intimacy must go hand in hand, because we owe our lovers the right to be with people of creativity and variety. Husbands tell me that the women at the office are sometimes more interesting simply because they are keeping up, following their muses, being stimulated, having their assumptions challenged, whereas their wives have become intellectually lazy, reading romances and watching television soap operas.

I once knew a university professor who was the soul of loyalty and who had always adhered to traditional values despite the fact that he wore jeans and pastel sweaters to class and always had a flock of young women who gazed at him with adulation while he lectured. Then, after being straight arrow for all those years, he suddenly found himself in love with a student and carrying on a torrid affair with her. When he came to see me, he was fighting to get out of the cauldron and to rebuild something with his wife.

Here was a man who jogged and played handball, took classes in sculpting, and worked hard at his profession. In short, he had stayed alert and alive. His wife, however, had not kept up. She had gained twenty pounds and had neglected her clothing and her appearance. The children had moved out on their own, and she was bored with herself.

It was a terrible jolt for her to discover that her husband had taken a lover. At first it only made her withdraw more, feel sorry for herself, and cry most of the day. When she came in to see me, she was a mess.

I talked later that night to the husband. Was the new woman really that much better than his wife?

"Well, no," he said. "They are both beautiful women. They have different shapes, one is blond and the other is brunette, and of course Jill is younger, but they are both terrific. I am a fortunate guy to have two wonderful women interested in me. The only real difference is that Jill is more alive. My wife used to be wide awake and liked to do things. She is bright, and really I still love her. It's just that she has not taken care of herself. Intellectually, physically, any way. She drinks two or three glasses of wine and is in a stupor every evening."

It's wonderful what resources people can draw on when their domain is threatened. Two weeks later I saw the wife, and she was a transformed woman. She had lost seven pounds, had a new hairstyle, and said to me, "I realize now that if I'm going to stay attractive for Bill I've got to develop myself. I don't know what got into me, but I've fallen asleep these last two years. It was not that I had stopped loving Bill. I had stopped respecting myself! It's a great big beautiful world out there, and there's a lot to see and do."

Obviously a wife who gets interested in life again becomes interesting. My friend the professor fell in love all over again, dropped the student, and is quite happily married now.

The Need for Creativity

Don't let anyone tell you that if you develop your own interests and hobbies it will be detrimental to your marriage. Within limits, if you find fields of endeavor at which you can excel, you give your mate a great deal by pursuing those gifts. We have a God-given need for creativity, for instance. Erik Erikson calls it the need for "generativity." Mothers with children have that in abundance when their children are young, but as our life situations change we all need to replace the voids in our lives with ways of being creative. Dr. Neil Warren, head of the Fuller Graduate School of Psychology, says of his wife Marylyn, "The thing that turns me on most about my wife is when she is pleased with herself. When she's happy, and enjoying her life, I enjoy her most."

Too Much Togetherness

It is curious that too much togetherness can be inimical to a strong self-image and therefore can be inimical to a strong love affair.

"I can't understand it," bemoaned a husband in my office. "We have some of our worst fights when we get home from a wonderful, intimate weekend together. After being together at some resort hotel, having great sex and lots of fun together, why would we get into such violent arguments?"

There could be many reasons, of course, but such fights can often erupt because one or both need some solitude and unconsciously ask for space by having an argument. Sure enough, when I talked to this man's wife the next week, she said, "Now that we are married, we seem to be Bobbsey Twins. Every time I tell Bob that I'm going to get up early and go jogging the next morning, he sets his alarm so he can go with me. But sometimes I want to go running alone!" That couple is headed for trouble if they do not negotiate a way of combining both intimacy and solitude, to keep their love, in Gibran's words, from being a "bond," but rather make it "a moving sea between the shores of [their] souls."[61]

Being married to a person doesn't mean that you must be wired together, every piece of your behavior influencing the behavior of your mate. Some people need a half-hour alone with a cup of coffee in the morning. Physician counselor Paul Tournier is an artist at love, yet he builds a stout wall around his daily hour for communion with God. It might seem, when some troubled patients need him, or when his family asks for time, that he would forgo that hour of meditation. But no. Tournier says that to maintan an ability to love, it is essential to have that quiet time.

The principle can be carried too far, of course. We all have known marriages that fractured over one or the other spending too much time away. We must strike a middle ground.

"I don't know what to do," wails Charlie Brown to his nemesis, Lucy. "Sometimes I get so lonely I can hardly stand it. Other times I actually long to be completely alone." Says a no-nonsense Lucy, "Try to live in-between. Five cents please."

Friends Outside the Marriage

Part of our strategy for strengthening self-esteem, and thus strengthening our love lives, should be to widen our circle of friends. In Samuel Johnson's phrase, to keep our friendships "in good repair." Here again, some of this probably needs to be done independently. As I said in an earlier book,[62] we make a terrible mistake to drop our old friends at the altar and to suppose that our socializing from that point on should be exclusively with other couples. The odds of four people all liking each other equally are not very good, and if your mate does not find much in common with your old friends, that should not halt the friendships. If you happen to find some other couple with whom you are *simpatico*, that's wonderful, but if not, you should not feel guilty about cultivating friendships on your own that meet your emotional needs and keep you stretching. I get uneasy when a man says to me, "My wife is my best friend. I can tell her everything, so I don't need other close friends." Your mate should be your best friend, but not your only friend. There is no way that any one person can meet all your emotional needs, and to expect your mate to do so is to put undue pressure on the relationship. If you surround yourself with supportive and healthy friendships in which you are stimulated to expand your horizons, you should arrive home from such associations happy. And most of us find it easiest to love when we are happiest.

Complementing Each Other

Love can last between two people who are quite different, and who continue to bring together aspects of their personalities that complement their mates' personalities.

When Ariel Durant died, she had been married to the famous scholar Dr. Will Durant for sixty-eight years. He was in intensive care at Cedars-Sinai Hospital at the time, being ninety-six, and supposedly was not informed of her death. But as columnist Jack Smith speculated, he must have sensed her passing and "would not have wanted her to go that far away without him."[63] At any rate, he died just two weeks later.

Diane and I had met the Durants at a book party a few years earlier. By this time they had become a very famous team, and I was eager to see how they looked and how they were with each other. He was surprisingly short, with a distinguished gray moustache. She was even shorter, peeking over his shoulder like some inquisitive bird. All of us knew the story of their wedding day—how she had roller-skated down from Harlem and met him at City Hall, "flushed and sweaty, with a torn stocking and a skinned knee," carrying her skates over her shoulder. He was twenty-seven, and she was fifteen.

Plenty of people predicted that such a preposterous match would not work, and indeed they were in some ways very different in temperament as well as in age. He was working on a doctorate at Columbia, and when they attended social functions she was poorly dressed and felt uncomfortable around the alert graduate students and their chic, well-educated girlfriends. But Will assured her that she was the best thing that had ever happened to him.

He was right. Although Ariel never bothered to finish college, she held four honorary doctorates the day we met. And her research and writing had become so important to Will that the two had been listed as co-authors of the last five volumes of his monumental series, *The Story of Civilization.* It is a reassuring picture to imagine them, married more than sixty years, as they sat in the library of their Hollywood Hills home, working on some historical passage.

Much of the secret of their superb mingling is that neither sacrificed his or her individuality, and each had singular things to contribute to the relationship. After they had been married more than fifty years, they began work on *A Dual Autobiography,* in which they wrote alternating chapters discussing their long lives together. Ariel, looking back on their meeting, says that she wondered how she, "a poor

Jewish girl, with nothing to offer but her body and her eager but poorly furnished mind," could attract this brilliant scholar. And in response, he writes,

Now I will tell you, Ariel. I had been buried in books and you came to me as the breath of life.... I loved your round arms, your shapely legs, your disheveled hair, your laughing eyes, your leaping breasts. I loved your agile mind, so eager to grow and learn and understand.[64]

Watching that frail little couple at the party, seeing how mutually interdependent they had become and how tenderly they treated each other, it was easy to believe that love can last.

The door to happiness swings outward.

—SØREN KIERKEGAARD

We have no more right to consume happiness without producing it than to consume wealth without producing it.

—GEORGE BERNARD SHAW

One does not "find oneself" by pursuing one's self, but on the contrary by pursuing something else and learning through discipline or routine—even the routine of making beds—who one is and wants to be.

—MAY SARTON

The paradox of love is that it is the highest degree of awareness of the self as a person and the highest degree of absorption in the other.

—ROLLO MAY

Let him who cannot be alone beware of community. . . . Let him who is not in community beware of being alone.

—DIETRICH BONHOEFFER

The Dangers of Looking Out for Number One

One reason love grows dim with the years is simple indifference. To make matters worse, an increasing self-centeredness sometimes accompanies that indifference. For example, Art Sueltz has satirized a common marriage problem by chronicling the stages of the common cold in seven years of marriage:

First year: "Sugar, I'm worried about my little baby girl. You've got a bad sniffle. I want to put you in the hospital for a complete checkup. I know the food is lousy, but I've arranged for your meals to be sent up from Rossini's."

Second year: "Listen, honey, I don't like the sound of that cough. I've called Dr. Miller and he's going to rush right over.

Now will you go to bed like a good girl just for me, please?"

Third year: "Maybe you'd better lie down, honey. Nothing like a little rest if you're feeling bad. I'll bring you something to eat. Have we got any soup in the house?"

Fourth year: "Look, dear. Be sensible. After you've fed the kids and washed the dishes, you'd better hit the sack."

Fifth year: "Why don't you take a couple of aspirin?"

Sixth year: "If you'd just gargle or something instead of sitting around barking like a seal."

Seventh year: "For heaven's sake, stop sneezing. What are you trying to do, give me pneumonia?"[65]

In the preceding chapter, I said that love often dies because people do not grow as individuals—they allow their self-images to deteriorate. But now I must discuss the danger of going too far the other way. Today we are seeing a caricature of self-confidence, the posturing and preening of those who have made Egotism a way of life. If the Caspar Milquetoasts of the world are incapacitated for love, the egomaniacs are even worse.

It may seem an oversimplification, but many marriages fail simply because one or both of the lovers are too self-centered. We can hope the booming me-ism of the last decade is subsiding, for we can see around us many wounded refugees who not long ago announced to their families and to the world, "I'm going to start taking care of *me* for a change." Then they discovered rather quickly that such preoccupation with the self can leave one very lonely, and that we were evidently made for something higher than inspecting our own navels.

This grossly distorted individualism can be laid at the doorstep of pop psychologists such as Robert Ringer (whose book titles have become veritable slogans for our culture—*Looking Out for Number One* and *Winning Through*

Intimidation) and Dr. Fritz Perls, whose testy credo can be found hanging on the waiting room walls of hundreds of American psychotherapists, presumably informing the love lives of their patients:

> I do my thing, and you do your thing.
> I am not in this world to live up to your expectations.
> And you are not in this world to live up to mine.
> You are you and I am I,
> And if by chance we find each other, it's beautiful.
> If not, it can't be helped.[66]

Such an idiosyncratic way of living has its attractions, but adherents of that philosophy should at least refrain from marrying and bearing children. Perls's wife and two children, whom he abandoned, did not feel that they benefited from his egocentrism.

The fact of the matter is that arrogance doesn't make for loving relationships. It may make you interesting—Fritz Perls was never dull—but it cripples your ability to love.

The Problem of Pride

The sort of arrogance I am discussing would have been described in earlier days as pride. And perhaps pride is a category that needs to be taken off the shelf and dusted off for use again. According to the older theologians, pride was the greatest sin because it was the root of all other sins. As I sit in my counseling room watching the carnage created by the uncoupling of two people who thrash and flail about while they "assert themselves," I realize that the older theologians had a point. There is already too much tendency within us to become self-absorbed, and we have not been aided by Ringer and Perls, who *encourage* the tendency.

Self-Transcendence

The alternative is self-transcendence. To find fullest meaning in life, we must be at peace with ourselves, but we must also get outside ourselves. When the Jewish psychiatrist Victor Frankl was in Nazi prison camps, what gave meaning to his life was the image of his wife, which was somehow more real and vivid in his mind than the reality of his prisoner's existence. It is not surprising that Frankl frequently asks his patients who are struggling with their sufferings: "For whose sake do you do so?" It is only when they begin to live for someone beyond themselves, Frankl contends, that they find happiness.[67]

Jesus nowhere urges self-contempt, but neither does he advocate self-worship, as do certain humanistic psychologists. We are to keep always before us a clear vision of the Holy ("You shall love the Lord your God with all your heart, and with all your soul, and with all your mind"). And we are to get outside our own skin by loving another ("You shall love your neighbor as yourself").[68]

How do the application of these principles make us better lovers and prevent the death of romance? In this, quite simply: we attend at least as closely to the needs of our mates as to our own. Every good lover I've ever known has developed a finely tuned sensitivity to others, and is regularly, attentively, aggressively noticing what makes his or her mate happy.

So Guideline Number Three for preventing the death of love is this:

> *Construct a balanced relationship*

I have two very strong, very different friends who are married to each other and have been very successfully contributing to each other's happiness for thirty-nine years. Dr. Dean Foster, who teaches at Virginia Military Institute in Lexington, Virginia, is one of the great eccentrics of the world. He is given to making outrageous remarks to strangers and is always immersed in a dozen research projects. He is a self-starter and a self-fulfilled man if ever there was one.

Such wizards who stay in their laboratories for days and nights on end do not ordinarily make good marriages, but he and Maxine are well coupled. One reason is that Maxine is exceedingly tolerant of the genius to whom she is married. The other is that Dean pays at least as much attention to her needs as to his own. For instance, Maxine is a painter, and Dean keeps careful track of her fluctuating interest in painting. Perhaps she will go for weeks without needing to take her brush in hand, but then he is suddenly aware of a change, sometimes without her saying a thing. It is time for her to spend a day in the Shenandoah Mountains with her easel. When the twins were young, Dean would drop his projects for the day and stay home with them and their diapers. I have seen him almost literally push her out the door with her supplies, heedless of her protestations. The important thing *that* day is that Maxine be able to paint. At other times, he goes along, carrying her box and easel, standing idly by, watching her work. One day I accompanied them, and it was a lesson in concentration to see how he watched her. He was as intensely absorbed as when immersed in a research project in his lab, and obviously taking pleasure in her success.

Here is a man who has a rich and full life, who is self-possessed and self-propelled. Yet he can transcend himself in the presence of Maxine and jumps on her bandwagon with great gusto. He is her best booster.

On Knowing Your Mate's Needs

Dean is able to encourage his wife because he knows her needs well. He has obviously undertaken to know the intricacies of her personality as he knows the intricacies of his laboratory. Not many of us pay that much attention.

I talked once to a young man who was not getting along well with his bride.

"How well do you know your wife?" I asked.

"Who *does* understand women?" he replied with a curled lip.

Getting to know a woman, I told him, is not very different from gaining information in any other field. He happened to be a real estate appraiser. Because his profession was research, I urged that he apply the principles from his field in trying to understand his wife.

A month later, when we had lunch together, I was a little startled by the literal way he had taken my suggestion. Something in what I'd said had rung a bell, and he went about researching his wife with the same enthusiasm and thoroughness that he studied an apartment building. He talked to her family about her childhood and now knew more about her roots and her upbringing. He even interviewed other people about her—asked her friends about her preferences and the gifts she might like. One week he took three days off from work to do all the housework and child care with her and to sit with her in class and listen to a day of lectures at her college. Each evening he paid attention to the information going into her computer—the things she read and the television programs she liked. In short, he immersed himself in his wife's life in order to understand her. In their case, at least, it was a successful experiment, and she was very flattered.

The Desire to Make Another Person Happy

What we are talking about, of course, is the heart of love: a desire to make another happy. It is the surest sign that you are in love when you find yourself planning and scheming ways to bring happiness to another. It is well-illustrated by a man who had fallen newly in love with a golden woman who was an ex-cheerleader and from whom emanated an energetic, moving, sensual allure. He said to me, "In my fantasies about her, it's not so much sex with her that I long for, although that's certainly part of it. More than anything else, it's a desire to make her happy. I fantasize about strolling down Fifth Avenue with her on a fall day, buying a hot pretzel from a vendor, and then seeing the delight in her face as she eats it. That's love for me—doing things that would make her happy."

Most people who have been soundly in love have had that overpowering desire to make the beloved happy, even if it requires some sacrifice. The sacrifice does not seem to matter, because they are getting their happiness from seeing the pleasure of the people they love. When this happens in your own relationship, you have experienced not only one of the greatest ecstasies possible in this life, but also a perfect example of the Christian ethic at work. You have transcended your self.

Providing Ecstasy for Your Mate

I notice that the people who enjoy ecstatic love pay very close attention to the need systems of their mates. They know exactly what things, what experiences, what enjoyments will bring pleasure to their beloved, and they do everything possible to provide those opportunities—even when those pleasures do not originate with them. It is one thing if a man's wife has ecstasy when she is in bed with him. That is very flattering to his ego. But it is another category altogether when his wife receives pleasure in some activity in which he does not participate.

Dr. Edward Danks is a Presbyterian pastor in Darien, Connecticut. He is a man who thinks everything through very carefully and is the soul of rationality. I suppose that he is Presbyterian partly for that reason: his sense of propriety and reason would make him curious about the more pietistic or enthusiastic Christian groups, but he would be uneasy being their pastor.

I asked him once what he thought of the whole neopentecostal movement, expecting a carefully reasoned rebuttal to their position. Instead, he said, "I've got to be tolerant of charismatics because I sleep with one!" Then he went on to describe how the experience of the Baptism of the Holy Spirit had come to his wife, Barbara, and what it meant to her. Although he did not fully understand her speaking in tongues, it made him happy to see her so happy.

Putting myself in his shoes, I think I might have done what many husbands do when their wives get into some new enthusiasm: put a damper on it. Explain to her that she may get disillusioned when the new wears off. Dissuade her. What we are really saying to our wives when we do that, of course, is that we don't like it when they don't get their happiness from us.

But not Ed. As foreign as the pentecostal experience was to him, he encouraged his wife to pursue it. He was nonjudgmental, and he even went beyond being nonjudgmental: he became her chief supporter. She attended a national charismatic conference at his suggestion. Then they sponsored an area meeting of neo-pentecostals in his own church. Why? Because he loved his wife, and anything that would enhance her life was worth his pursuing. What he was practicing, consciously or unconsciously, was William James's rule: do not interfere with another's peculiar ways of being happy, provided those ways do not interfere by violence with yours.

In these chapters, I have been discussing two extremes, both of which contribute to the death of love. The first is self-depreciation, which leads to neurotic dependency. The second is self-aggrandizement, which leads to arrogance. It is the difference between Woody Allen, who says, "Pardon me for being this way," and Mohammed Ali, who says, "I am the King."

Somewhere between these two extremes lies the golden mean. Perhaps the answer is in that deceptively simple remark made by the greatest psychologist of all time, Jesus, when asked about the great commandments. We must do two things, he said: love God and love our neighbor as ourself. By obeying the first, we acquire a balanced perspective on the self. When one is at worship it is impossible to engage in either arrogance or self-contempt. The paradox of the second command is that we discover ourselves best while loving another.

Friendship is seldom lasting but between equals. . . . Benefits which cannot be repaid and obligations which cannot be discharged are not commonly found to increase affection. They excite gratitude indeed and heighten veneration, but commonly take away that easy freedom and familiarity of intercourse without which . . . there cannot be Friendship.

—SAMUEL JOHNSON

In the all-important world of family relations, there are other words almost as powerful as the famous "I love you." They are "Maybe you're right."

—OREN ARNOLD

Love is seldom spontaneous, instant, dynamic. It usually takes considerable time to create. It results from work, from thinking, from promoting equality, from being able to cope and adapt.

—WILLIAM LEDERER

Love, Honor, and Negotiate

Most of us know a family in which the system is fairly well in balance and the marriage goes along well for many years, but then suddenly the center does not hold and things blow apart with a centrifugal force. What has frequently happened is that one partner's needs have changed rapidly and the other partner did not keep up with those shifting needs. Let's say a husband is an alcoholic. The marriage is a mess, and everyone wonders why she puts up with it. Usually there is a certain trade off for her. She is sacrificing, but somewhere in the system she is getting compensated.

But let's say, the husband suddenly goes on the wagon. Now he's not drinking any more, and she can't be the martyr any longer. More often than we might expect, a divorce occurs at this point. Why? Because the marriage could not equalize itself quickly enough.

Here is another illustration. One partner is considerably overweight. Let's assume that it is the wife. When one of the partners is fat, that has been considered, perhaps unconsciously, in setting up the balance. Often she attempts to buy love through acquiescence, feeling that she must in some way make up for her unattractiveness. Now she loses a lot of weight and is looking terrific. Gone is her "don't-make-waves-he-may-throw-me-out" policy, and in its place comes a new pride. She is aware of her rights and now tends to speak up more. The system must make some very large adjustments. For some, it is too much too fast. Without ever realizing why it happened, they find themselves splitting apart.

Adjusting to Shifts in Needs

Most marriages are based on a group of assumptions about what two people want from each other. Perhaps such information was quite accurate for the early years, but it is a mistake to assume that your mate's needs today are the same as they were ten years ago. A woman who was happy to stay home and rear the children earlier may have completely different desires today. Similarly, power needs that a husband expressed in his twenties may shift radically in his middle years, and he may no longer want to be so independent. In fact, as psychiatrist C. G. Jung has pointed out, a man's and a woman's needs may cross during the important middle years. The woman is now ready to invade the outside world and make a mark for herself, whereas the man is now weary of that arena of competition and striving. He wants to be home more, to develop his nurturing, feminine side.

Perhaps too much has been made of "midlife crises" in the recent literature, but I find in my work with couples that it is very important to get them to look at such changes going on in their lovers. Chores that were once simple can become very irritating. Let's take the simple illustration of who pays the bills. Perhaps a couple decided a long time ago that the husband would be responsible for that. She didn't care, and he was willing, so she was glad to have him take over the bills. But now it is five years later, and every time he has to sit down to write out the checks he fumes and fusses and is in a foul mood for twenty-four hours afterward. One would think that the signs are apparent that some reshuffling may be needed here. But she too easily assumes that she knows her husband, and that this irritation is not to be taken seriously, because he was the one who wanted to pay the bills. Such a situation can blow into a serious point of contention, although she would be quite willing to take over the bills if only she knew. Both partners are probably to blame here. She is at blame for not investigating. And he is at fault for not saying to her, "Honey, these sessions with the checkbook are getting me down, and I can't seem to cope with all this juggling of the bills. I probably take it out on you by screaming every two weeks about how much money this family is spending, when I'm really just fed up with this rotten chore. Would you mind doing it for a while?"

Perhaps there will have to be a trade-off for this shift to work. I know a couple who were both very unhappy with their duties, so they made a radical shift. He now does all the grocery shopping and cooking; she does all the yard work and washes the dishes. Such an arrangement may sound unacceptable to many couples, but that's not the point. The important thing is that those two talked to each other about what they like, what they enjoy, and what bugs them. And they were open to change.

I do not mean to say that marriage can be some perfect state where one person only does the things he or she wants to do and the other takes up the slack. Life is a series of compromises, and every successful marriage I know involves putting up with things you don't like. What I *do* mean to say is that as the shifts occur you can renegotiate the relationship and the way you are supplying each other's needs.

Which brings me to Suggestion Number Four.

> *Regularly renegotiate with your lover*
> *the exchanges in your relationship*

The idea of negotiating and renegotiating may sound too mercantile for such a matter of the heart as love. But I notice that without calling it that, most happily adjusted couples have a way of adjusting the balance. If one is getting more than he or she is giving, the system is rearranged.

When two people fall in love, they usually do so because a large chunk of their needs are being met by the other person. At first they feel so good when they're with each other. Their sexual needs are being filled, they feel happier than ever before. It's wonderful.

But now let's say they are eight years into the marriage. He still loves his wife, but he's not happy. The job is frustrating, and he'd like to move to Oregon. She doesn't like rain, and the idea of selling the house and gambling on a new future scares her. Besides, she's attached to her parents, who live nearby.

What we have now is two need systems starting on a collision course. The plot thickens when we learn that she'd like to have children and he says they can't afford a family yet. She does not say so when the Oregon subject comes up, but part of her reluctance to pull up stakes is that she assumes it would entail postponing a family. Oregon becomes a subject they can't discuss.

He dreads going to work more and more, and on the way home he's now stopping for a few beers. When he gets home he has a few more and falls asleep on the floor while watching television. Sometimes she wakes him up to go to bed. At other times, she lets him lie there and wanders into the bedroom alone. Their sex life, which at one time was terrific, is now less passionate and less frequent. He has gained weight and feels self-conscious about his belly hanging over her when they make love. Because he is ignoring her sexually, she, in turn, feels unattractive.

So the system deteriorates.

A marriage counselor troubleshooting the matter ought to be able to see that the Oregon question is a mess and that many of the underlying difficulties and resentments occurred because of misunderstandings there. The amazing thing is that the Oregon matter was never fully discussed to see if some compromise were possible. Instead, he half-heartedly talked about it, not revealing how much he hated his job. And when he talked about it, she laughed a little and changed the subject. He, in turn, pulled back, hurt. And she went her way never realizing how much he was dreaming of making a move. Strangely, when the topic was raised when friends were visiting, he displayed harsh anger.

How do we solve such conflicts? By negotiation and compromise. In this case, for instance, it may be that she would be very happy to move if he would be willing to start a family as soon as they're settled. Or perhaps he would be happy to stay where they are if he could change jobs but has hesitated to bring that topic up for fear that she will think him a quitter.

Simple solutions are not available for every marital disagreement. But it is imperative that two people acquire the habit of regularly sharing their dreams and their frustrations with each other, listening carefully to the changes going on in their mates, and sitting down to do some serious problem solving.

Love as Equality

Here is a couple in their middle forties. Their daughter has just made them grandparents, and their fifteen-year-old son is still at home. During the early years, Martha was busy with Scouts, Little League, and PTA, while Bob was busy building a small plumbing business. When the children were small, the two slipped away as often as possible to do such things as having a quiet picnic in the park. One day they checked into a motel with a bag of chocolate-covered peanuts and alternately made love and ate candy.

When all the children were in school, Martha enrolled at the local university and eventually finished four years of college and two years of graduate school in the field of social work. When she was in school, Bob and the children pitched in with the chores at home and they cheered wildly when she received her diploma. Now she works as a social worker at a family service agency and loves her work.

Through the years, Martha and Bob have had periods when they wished they'd never met, never married, and especially never had children. At times Bob has been angry about his disintegrating income after paying tuition bills, and sometimes has thought wistfully of a lovely South Sea island where he could take up beachcombing. Martha has occasionally gone off by herself for a good cry, and sometimes for a weekend or a day she has completely turned her back on her family and on their various needs and demands.

They've also learned that their relationship has changed from wildly exciting to warmly glowing—with an occasional exciting flash. And they can laugh together over the change in their responses to one another. Through it all, they have maintained their sense of humor, and they have both been ready to change in order to adjust to each other's needs. Bob, for instance, has recently enrolled in the same university from which Martha got her degree and in which their daughter is now a part-time student. To the amazement of his children, he has bought a motorcycle, to save both gasoline and time. He jauntily straddles it every morning and zooms off past their neighbors, while they watch him with envy and some perplexity. Martha is very happy that Bob is actively in the process of changing, and she is willing to shoulder a major part of the family's financial responsibilities while her husband gets a college degree.

Neither has had any extramarital sexual affairs. And neither has a clear-cut plan for what he or she will be doing ten years from now, but they're committed to adjusting to each other.[69] Theirs is a good example of a marriage that is regularly renegotiating and readjusting itself.

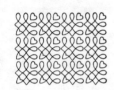

PART IV

*Sixteen Ways to Weather
Marital Storms Without
Sinking the Ship*

People are not always very tolerant of the tears which they themselves have provoked.

—PROUST

Never to be angry, never to disagree at all seems to most of us a sign not of love but of indifference.

—ALLAN FROMME

A marriage is like a long trip in a tiny row boat: if one passenger starts to rock the boat, the other has to steady it; otherwise, they will go to the bottom together.

—DAVID REUBEN

A man should sleep sometime between lunch and dinner in order to be at his best in the evening when he joins his wife and friends at dinner. My wife and I tried two or three times in the last forty years to have breakfast together, but it was so disagreeable we had to stop.

—WINSTON CHURCHILL

Conflict and How to Defuse It

We must now discuss the turbulent periods through which many marriages sooner or later pass, when the balanced system blows up and the partners are fighting so violently that no one's needs are being met.

Here are some suggestions for handling conflict:

1. *Allow for temporary insanity in your mate.* Any two people who have associated closely enough for long enough are sure to hit some turbulence in the relationship. The best marriages have a built-in allowance for such storms. If you have agreed beforehand that a husband and wife who love each other deeply will probably experience some envy, annoyance, boredom, even anger, then neither of you will panic when it happens.

I often speak to management and sales groups on the topic, "How to bring out the best in people," and one of my suggestions is to allow for periods of temporary insanity in one's business partners. All of us wander along the borders of irrationality, and most people cross over that line from time to time. At least I do. But I'm very fortunate that I work with an exceptionally tolerant man. Dr. Taz Kinney, my associate, smiles benevolently when I'm emotionally out of commission for a few days. He knows from experience that I'll be back and that later the tables may be reversed, when he will need to take more than he gives.

The same principle applies to marriage. If you allow for some storms, expect some turbulence, and do not jump ship, a divorce will usually not be necessary. "Love is patient," according to the Apostle Paul. Betty Ford calls it "the art of generous compromise." When she and Gerald Ford planned to marry, they had long talks about what they expected from each other. "In a very businesslike way," says Mrs. Ford, "we defined our objectives. We decided, for example, on the number of children. We decided too, that a successful marriage is never really the 50–50 proposition it's talked up to be. We settled for a 75–25 deal. Sometimes the 75 would emanate from my side. Sometimes it would have to be Jerry's gesture."[70]

2. *Recognize that anger is a normal emotion.* Nobody likes anger, but we can learn to accept it as a normal expression both in ourselves and in our mates.

Sometimes we are programmed from the past to have an unreasonable fear of all negative feelings. I talked to a patient who had been married three times and we determined to get to the bottom of his difficulties with women. One afternoon he came in after having lunch with a girlfriend. He was ecstatic about the disagreement they'd had at lunch.

"It was terriffic," he said. "For the first time I can re-member, I got mad at a woman and we worked it out. Before lunch was finished, we were friends again. In the past, when I ventilated any displeasure (which was rare), they would turn on me or go away and pout."

I probed a bit, for I couldn't believe that *all* of these women in his life had handled his anger so badly.

"Were you allowed to blow up as a kid?" I asked.

"When I did," he replied, "I paid a price for it. My mom would get hurt and withdraw. Then I'd feel so guilty."

He pondered before going on. "I remember going to my room and thinking, 'I sure must be bad to hurt my mom so much.'"

It was not difficult to see, then, why he was so afraid of his anger, and why he assumed that women were reacting to it with more rejection than actually was present.

There are other reasons we panic unnaturally at the ap-pearance of conflict. Perhaps our parents quarrelled exces-sively, and we decided that we would never allow such feelings in our own marriage. Or perhaps an experience with a former lover has discolored our ability to tolerate the normal upheavals of a healthy relationship.

Whatever the causes for swallowing our anger, we must overcome them, for repressed hostility can lead to dimin-ished sex drive, extramarital affairs, and lots of other seem-ingly inexplicable behavior. When a man says to me, "My wife is a terrific person, but I'm going to have to divorce her because I don't love her any more," or when a woman says, "I don't know what's wrong with me, but I can't stand to have my husband touch me these days," my first ques-tion is, "What are you angry about?"

3. *Assume the best about your mate.* Signals do get scrambled

occasionally, and it is smart to assume the best instead of the worst. Until you're proven wrong, believe that your partner and you have misunderstood each other, and that he or she is not out to hurt you.

Here is a young couple who have recently married. Several times, after they've gone to bed, there is a discussion about locking the doors.

"Did you lock the door?"

"No, I thought you did."

And so someone pads off to do the chore. It is only a minor irritant, but it builds up, and finally one night there's a scene. They accuse each other of being inconsiderate and of taking advantage. Not until breakfast, when things are calmed down slightly, do this bride and groom discover the problem. In her family, her father always locked up. When he was growing up, that job belonged to his mother. Each assumed that the other mate knew it was his or her job and was being stubborn.

In miniature, that incident displays how resentment can begin to spread in a marriage. Two people are building on certain false assumptions, and when things go awry they assume malicious motives about each other. Better to assume the best and look for the scrambled message.

4. *When your mate snarls, check to see if the cause is hurt rather than anger.*

Anger and pain are very easily confused. When an animal is injured and you try to help, the animal often snarls. Not because it is angry at you, but because it is in pain and is afraid that you are going to hurt it more.

It is a safe assumption, when dealing with ill-feeling coming from your partner, that the emotion originates in hurt rather than in ill-will toward you. The sooner each of you can learn to say, "I'm feeling hurt" instead of snarling, the better your love will work. In the meantime, look for the injured paw before snarling back.

5. *Recognize that your mate's unhappiness is not always your responsibility.* Here again, before leaping to assumptions about your marriage being in trouble, ascertain the cause of your partner's unhappiness. It may have nothing to do with you.

Too frequently we get angry at our lovers for being angry. We don't like anyone upsetting the tranquility of our homes, and we want people to be cheerful when we're around. Such a blissful state would be nice, but it's not very realistic. Married couples do well to have an understanding that each is going to be a little miserable at times. It may be that he or she is distressed with a boss, or bugged by someone at school, or suffering from a sour stomach. In such states, your lover may not be able to express much affection for you, but that temporary incapacity is not your fault. The two questions to ask are "Honey, have I done something to make you angry?" If the answer to that is no, the second is "Then is there anything I can do for you?" If not, you are free to leave your lover alone. And by giving him or her the right to an occasional funk, you have transmitted a wonderful gift.

6. *Be cautious about protecting your turf.* Throughout this book, I have been saying that it is reasonable to enter a marriage with the hope that certain needs for love will be met and that there is nothing selfish about approaching your husband or wife with an unfulfilled desire. But I must mitigate that a bit now by saying that some people are so jumpy about keeping their share that they get trigger-happy. We all know people who go through life spending most of their available emotional energy in self-defending action. That quality makes for very little love. Secure peo-

ple, on the other hand, do not see every misunderstanding as an occasion to "assert themselves" and protect their turf. They are able to compromise and give up some ground here and there without losing any self-composure. In short, they are relating to others out of their strength rather than their weakness.

7. *Give your partner the right to possess contradictory emotions.* We tend to look at love very simply and to ask our mates to be either one way or the other. Let's say the primary question in his mind is "Does she love me or does she not?" One day she explodes and says, "No, I don't love you!" He may then throw up his hands and conclude that there's nothing left to do but draw up the divorce papers.

In fact, our feelings are rarely black or white about anything. We are, rather, a complex mixture of many emotions. On some days, one feeling is dominant; another day, some other feeling. The fact that your husband does not feel loving toward you today does not mean that he has "fallen out of love." It may be that he is so angry at you today for forgetting to cancel his dentist appointment that all he can think of is the $25 fee. But today's anger does not mean that he won't feel warm and loving toward you tomorrow.

In other words, it is a grave mistake to assume that a partner's emotional life is either fixed or one-dimensional. Alan Paton, the great South African novelist, describes the interior of the soul aptly:

This discovery of the complexity of human nature was accompanied by another—the discovery of the complexity and irrationality of human motive, the discovery that one could love and hate simultaneously, be honest and cheap, be arrogant and humble, be any pair of opposites that one had supposed to be mutually exclusive. This, I believe, is not common knowledge and would be incomprehensible to many. It has always been known, of course, by the dramatists and novelists. It is, in fact, a knowledge far more disturbing to other people than writers, for to writers it is the grist of their mills.[71]

8. *Change your patterns of relating.* One of the best results of family research in the last few years has been the application of general systems theory to family life. When two people marry, so the theory goes, those two individuals constitute a system. That system begins to have a life of its own and cause the parts to behave in ways they would not behave in isolation.

Counselors see the principle of systems operating every day. A patient I've come to know well during individual sessions may arrive for a joint session with his wife—and, behold, he is a totally different person. Of course, anyone who has watched certain married couples sees that. A woman talks and acts a certain way when her husband is in the room and another way when he is gone. It is not that she is being dishonest, it is simply that the relationship controls her behavior powerfully.

Looking back at my own marital stumblings, I realize that it never occurred to my first wife or me to look at our marriage as a system that we were constructing. We thought of ourselves as individuals, and if something went wrong between us, we thought that one or the other must be doing something wrong.

But in fact, when you've been with someone for a few years, you have accumulated memories of past problems and solutions, patterns of communication, hierarchies of power, and assumptions about right and wrong, all of which accumulate into a mass of data that the system is constantly scanning before acting. In our case, it turned out to be a weighty and ponderous mass.

At this point, a professional marriage counselor can sometimes help. If the marriage is not functioning, the system may be out of balance. Like an automobile engine, it occasionally needs a mechanic. There is nothing wrong with any of the parts: they simply need to be adjusted so that the mechanism runs smoothly again.

9. *Don't attempt to cure marital conflict with children.* One of our culture's myths is that couples get closer when a baby arrives. But there is overwhelming evidence to the contrary. Studies show that the central axis of the family—the husband and wife relationship—is bent or even broken by the presence of children. Couples report themselves happiest with each other before children are born and after they have left the nest.[72]

In a survey conducted by *Ladies Home Journal,* 72 percent of the women without children said they were satisfied with their marriages, while only 57 percent of those with children could agree. Mothers, compared to the childless wives,

- Were less satisfied with their lives in general (55 percent of women with children reported that they were happy, compared to 65 percent of the childless)
- Were less happy with their sex lives (26 percent as compared to 16 percent)
- Tired more easily (49 percent as compared to 43 percent)
- Felt angry and irritable more often (41 percent as compared to 31 percent)[73]

I am, of course, in favor of parenthood. The satisfactions of rearing children make up for the disadvantages as long as you have a solid relationship and are braced for the stress. But given the facts, it does not appear that you can cure marital discord by having a baby. Those who try usually find themselves with a troubled marriage plus a baby.

10. *Do not discuss divorce unless you mean it.* All too often, when things are stormy between two people, one will begin brandishing the possibility of divorce when all he or she is trying to do is convince the other that the situation is serious. It is a dangerous ploy. When you are feeling unheard and unattended to, you have a right to say that. But if you try to communicate your desperation by shock talk, you must be prepared for the possibility that your mate may stop trying then and there. Once two people begin discussing divorce, it is surprising how quickly they can be living in separate apartments. The tragedy of such a case is that the topic sometimes comes up, not because anyone was seriously considering it, but only because someone wanted to be loved.

I know a couple who have been married for more than fifty years. Their relationship has been very stormy at times. Theodore drank heavily for almost a decade, and both of them have even had some extramarital affairs. But all that is more than twenty years behind them, and they have a wonderful love affair going now. "The romance has come and gone," Sarah told me recently, "but there was never any question that we loved each other. And even when each of us had slipped badly in keeping our vows, we never considered divorce, and it never came up in any of our fights. We wanted to be married to each other, and as long as that was understood, we knew we could somehow get out of any mess we'd gotten ourselves into."

Marriage is a job. Happiness or unhappiness has nothing to do with it. There was never a marriage that could not be made a success, nor a marriage that could not have ended in bitterness and failure.

—KATHLEEN NORRIS

Be not angry that you cannot make others as you wish them to be, since you cannot make yourself as you wish to be.

—THOMAS À KEMPIS

Dear Abby: I am forty-four and would like to meet a man my age with no bad habits.—Rose
Dear Rose: So would I.

Reconciliation

I have been saying that a certain amount of fighting goes on in all healthy relationships. But when aggression gets out of control, the relationship can go into a destructive spin. Then the anger feeds on itself, and the marriage is in serious trouble. Here are some suggestions for halting that destructive spin:

1. *Resist the impulse to give up.* Many couples who come to a clinic like ours do so as a last resort. By the time they arrive, their relationship is in shreds. One would think that when two people have been badly hurt they would not have the energy to fight, but we often see people who seem to be locked into a fight to the death.

They are often ready to give up on the marriage and many therapists would not try to talk them out of it.

Working with such people is very draining work for the marriage counselor, and some of us are simply not up for it. Not wanting to get into the midst of a dogfight, the counselor may tell them that they are hurting each other and should pack it in. Or the counselor may say, "You both need help, and I'd be willing to see you each alone for therapy, but I'm not going to promise anything about your marriage. What you decide about divorcing or staying together will be up to you." It is an easy way out.

I do not wish to be harsh with my colleagues—none of us can tolerate an infinite amount of conflict. But perhaps because of my own divorce and because of my convictions about marriage, I try to salvage every marriage that comes in the door. Obviously, I don't win them all and in the end some of my patients decide to leave the relationship. But marriage is too sacred for me to recommend its dissolution. Ever. In most cases, the best marriage for a person is the one he or she is in, and no matter how great the anguish, any marriage can be saved. The key is motivation. If two people want to rebuild, if they want badly enough to love again, they can.

The easy way out, of course, is to throw in the towel and find a replacement. At first a new partner will seem to be everything that the old one was not. "I can talk to her," a man will say about his new girlfriend. "It's such a great feeling when I'm with her. I can tell her things I could never seem to tell my wife."

Just why is it so much easier for him to tell a new woman things he'd never tell his wife? Easy. It's because he has no history with this new woman. "We are inclined to believe those whom we do not know because they have never deceived us," said Samuel Johnson. With a stranger there is no accumulation of wounds, no topics that he has learned to avoid. In other words, it's a clean slate, and of course it's easier. But the ease of this new openness does not for a minute mean that there's something about this new woman that his wife does not have. All the new woman has is a clean slate.

Many of us are opposed to divorce as a matter of religious principle, but more and more experts who work with remarriages every day are opposing it for pragmatic reasons. Changing partners simply does not eliminate the problems. Dr. Irene Kassorla, author of *Nice Girls Do,* certainly not a religious moralist, is very down on divorce. She has two daughters and is divorced herself, but she says, "I really feel that marriage is an ideal human state and divorce is a waste of time. You just find the old partner with a new head."[74] All of us in this business have talked to hundreds of people who are having trouble in their second marriages and who say, "If I'd known then what I know now, I would have worked harder to keep that first marriage going. It wasn't all that bad."

2. *Believe that it can get better.* "Love hopes all things," wrote the Apostle Paul in his great hymn to love, and I notice that successful lovers are usually optimists about their relationship. It may not be going well at the moment, but they reach back to remember the good times, and they tenaciously hold on to the belief that it can get better again. All love relationships are something of a dance in which two people are constantly moving, sometimes coming close together and again moving away to gain some space. Occasionally, they may find themselves far apart, but that does not mean the dance is over. If they are patient and do not bolt, they can draw close together again.

When one embattled couple showed up at their pastor's study, they admitted that they were there only so they could say that they'd done everything possible. They had been married seven years, but during the last four they scarcely spoke except to discuss their daughter. She was the only thing they had in common.

"Their impasse," says Dr. D. L. Dykes, senior pastor of the First Methodist Church in Shreveport, Louisiana, "was that they saw only two alternatives: to stay together in the unhappy relationship they had, or to divorce. But they were reasonable people, willing to listen, and we showed them that there was still another way, that it was possible to make some changes."

Today those two are *very* happy together. The husband is fond of quoting from the story of the Prodigal Son, in which the father exults that his son "who once was dead, is now alive." Putting his arm around his wife, the husband smiles and says, "Our love once was dead, but boy is it alive now!"

Perhaps the man quotes the Bible a little out of context, but no matter. They have proved once again that love can return, that two people who genuinely want to rebuild a relationship can do so.

It is a mistake to take the fatalistic stance that your mate is intractable and that your marriage is doomed to remain a poor one. All living organisms are changing. People change and relationships can change.

Which brings us to Suggestion Number Three for breaking the destructive spin.

3. *Be the first to make a change.* Many couples get stuck in a pathological situation. They are caught in repetitive behavior that does not bring any solutions to their problems. What the therapist tries to do is to put some pressure on the marital system to get it unstuck. But often it is not necessary to call in an outside expert if one of you is willing to take some risks and experiment with something different.

But that is where the rub comes. We all have a certain resistance to change, a refusal to budge, otherwise known as pride. To change, we say, would be to admit that we are wrong. Yet we know that if we could begin afresh and change some things about the way we are relating, it just might break the log jam.

A woman came to Bruce Larson after he'd given a speech on reconciliation. "Can God heal a broken relationship that isn't just broken—it doesn't even exist?" she asked. When pressed for an explanation, she said, "My husband and I never quarrel and are never angry. We simply have no relationship. He comes home from work, has dinner, watches television, reads the paper, and then goes to bed. Later on, after I have read the paper and watched television, I go to bed."

"Is it like that every night?" Larson asked.

"Every night for years," she answered.

"Are you both Christians?"

"No, I'm a Christian, but my husband is not."

"Do you love him?"

"Yes," she said, tears beginning to form in her eyes. "I love him very much."

"Do you think he loves you?"

"No, I'm sure he doesn't or he wouldn't be so cold and indifferent."

"Well," Larson said, "as a Christian, you are the one who must be vulnerable and find out the true nature of your husband's feelings. He must love you, or he wouldn't be coming home to this dreadfully boring routine every night. He'd be out bowling or drinking or doing something a little more creative than what you describe. Perhaps he's hoping that one day something will happen to rekindle the love that you shared when you were first married."

"But what can I do?" the woman asked.

"What are you doing now to change the relationship?"

"I keep inviting him to our prayer group," she replied, "and I leave books and pamphlets around, hoping he will read them."

"Is it working?" Larson asked.

"No," she admitted.

"Then why don't you try something much more radical and costly to you? This is what the cross is all about. You must be vulnerable for your husband in the same way that Christ on the cross was vulnerable for you."

"Give me a for instance."

Larson says he grabbed for something wild. "Some night when he's watching television, why don't you put on your flimsiest lace nightie and your best perfume, jump into his lap and ruffle his hair, and tell him you love him as much as ever. What do you think his response would be?"

"I'd hate to guess," she giggled.

"But what's the worst thing that might happen if you took this step in faith?"

"He might laugh at me."

"That's true. And would that hurt?"

"It would hurt more than anything I can think of."

A few days later, when Bruce returned to his office, he received a letter from her that began, "Dear Bruce: I did what you suggested and guess what? He didn't laugh!"[75] It was the beginning of a new relationship between the two of them.

Of course it might not have turned out that way. When we take the initiative to be vulnerable and loving it usually does not have dramatic results, but it does make a powerful impression. I know of few relationships that cannot be turned around if just one person will swallow his or her pride and begin to let love work.

The next suggestion is closely allied to the preceding one.

4. *Cultivate humility.* "Love does not insist on its own way," says I Corinthians. Some husbands and wives are so caught up in being right all the time that they not only disagree with their mates, they annihilate them. That over-reaction may be due to a fear of losing control, a fear of being shown to be wrong. If so, that fear had best be eradicated as early as possible, for if you can never be wrong, you can never sustain love.

At a dinner party one night Lady Churchill was seated across the table from Sir Winston, who kept making his hand walk up and down—two fingers bent at the knuckles. The fingers appeared to be walking toward Lady Churchill. Finally, her dinner partner asked, "Why is Sir Winston looking at you so wistfully, and whatever is he doing with those two knuckles on the table?"

"That's simple," she replied. "We had a mild quarrel before we left home, and he is indicating it's his fault and he's on his knees to me in abject apology."[76]

Movies may succeed with the idea that love is never having to say you're sorry, but I've never known of a marriage to succeed on that premise. Most lovers have to say, "I'm sorry" a great deal. We need not think poorly of ourselves to say, "I'm sorry." Any two people who live closely are bound to bump into each other often, and when you're in love with another you do not want to hurt him or her, even with the little bumps. So you apologize.

Robert Fontaine wrote in *Atlantic Monthly* some time ago about visiting his elderly parents in their little apartment, chatting about baseball, drinking the tea his mother inevitably brewed for him. Their lives seemed so constricted.

I wondered, What do they think about? Do they notice each

other? Do they have strong emotions about each other? But how could they? The blood has slowed down. The arms are inelastic. The eyes are dim.

Yet one morning when I called, I found them fighting. They were bickering and shouting about some obscure matter, something to do with an event some twenty-five years previous. They had different ideas as to how the event turned out, and the discussion got hotter and hotter.

"That's the way you are, always so sure of yourself," my father said.

"I ought to know, I was there."

"I was there, too."

"Well, you don't remember then."

"My memory is perfect," my father shouted.

They kept at it like newlyweds for about fifteen minutes. Finally my father took his hat and rushed out of the apartment, slamming the door.

"Let him go," my mother said.

"I guess I'll have to. What were you fighting about?"

My mother shrugged. "I don't remember. He's just so stubborn. I keep hoping he'll outgrow it."

"If he hasn't now, he never will."

"Well, he better. I won't put up with it much longer."

Fontaine went home; then his mother called to say that his father had not yet returned. She was not as crisp as she had been. "I hope he doesn't do anything foolish," she said. "He's not a young man, you know."

Fontaine says it was "amazing to think of [my father], at his age, being sulky and irritated with my mother and she, for that matter, being wistful and lonesome like a girl at her first quarrel. In a way it was rather refreshing. I did not think that they had it in them." But he decided to walk over and keep his mother company until he returned.

She spoke as if it was all over and my father had deserted her for another woman. At last the door opened and my father walked calmly in. He had a small package in his hand. He smiled quietly and said, "Hello."

"Where've you been?" I asked. My mother was forced to smile. She was so glad to see him.

"I went to a movie. All in bright color. It hurt my eyes."

"You want some tea?" my mother asked. "You must be tired after all that color."

He handed her the package. It was a bottle of hand lotion, the sort that is guaranteed to make your hands soft as silk. My father hung his head a little and blushed. It was quite touching.

My mother beamed. "What a lovely bottle!"

"They say it keeps your hands like velvet," my father said.[77]

When things go wrong in our relationships, we have no reason to feel that we have failed. But when we lose our humility, a small disagreement can turn into a major conflagration.

5. *Add a large portion of tolerance.* I once saw this anonymous saying on a monastery wall: "Love is found by those who can live with human nature as it is." Those who most enjoy their love relationships are those who can relax with the faults and foibles of people. Asked about his long marriage to Joanne Woodward, Paul Newman said, "I don't think you can get impatient with each other. We are all flawed, and you've got to love each other enough so that those flaws aren't taken out of context."[78]

Some of the best marriages I know are between very different people—some of them with very striking idiosyncrasies—who are able to be magnanimously tolerant of each other. One professional man of my acquaintance has never been able to have sex with his wife in any place except the bedroom of their own home. When they travel, he is simply unable to perform.

"Doesn't that bother you?" I exclaimed to his wife.

She smiled benevolently and said, "No, not really. He's a wonderful man and a wonderful lover, and I could put up with larger oddities than this one when we love each other so much." I realized that it was a problem she had solved fine, thank you, and that as Dostoeveski somewhere says, we are a remarkably pliant animal. We can adjust to almost anything if we choose to.

And to choose to overlook the irritants and enjoy the good features of our mates is to choose a way of life that can bring great happiness. Dr. Carl Rogers, who is perhaps the best-known psychologist in America today, says that when he walks on the beach at La Jolla and enjoys the sunset, different every evening, he does not call out and say, "A little more orange over to the right, please," or "Would you mind giving us less purple in the back?" No, he enjoys the ever-changing, always-different sunsets as they are. We do well to do the same with the people we love.

6. *Decide to stop destroying and start building.* Any living organism such as marriage can sustain a certain amount of bruising, but like a plant, it requires watering and feeding in order to stay alive. There comes a point at which no organism can sustain an unlimited amount of tearing down. At some point in a troubled marriage, the couple should make a conscious decision that they will do nothing else to destroy it and that they will begin to do some specific things to nurture it.

Bill and Edie had drifted apart, and every discussion turned into an argument. "We were fighting," Edie says, "three, four times a week. And we were slinging mud."

Bill concurs, "It seemed as if we were grabbing for any ammunition with which we could hurt the other one. It was like living in a hell of reruns night after night."

Edie relates how it came to a head. "It was one of those days when everything went wrong, and we were letting off plenty of steam with each other. Then, all at once, in the middle of a tirade, Bill stopped and looked at me, and I looked at him, and we both realized a great truth: that in the middle of all this nonsense we were linked together. We had chosen each other, and there was a bridge between our souls. That night, we heated soup for the kids, ordered a pizza for ourselves, and made love in the living room to the strains of the 10 o'clock news."

Bill and Edie lived the next couple of weeks in near silence. "It was our own personal peace with honor," says Bill. "We determined to blow up no more bridges."

At that point in their marriage, only a thread held this couple together—a memory of a time when regardless of circumstances it only mattered that they had each other. The important thing was that they halted the destructive spin, determined, as Bill puts it, "to blow up no more bridges." That conscious turning point made an enormous difference for those two. They began to inventory what they had in common and what they could build on, then the friendship began to rebuild. That was several years ago, and they tell me that their friendship is more solid than ever.

Reconciliation can occur. With enough patience, and with enough commitment, anyone can rebuild. As we've been saying, the only thing necessary for reconstruction is two people who want it badly enough. If they do, their love may not return tomorrow, but it can return.

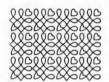

PART V

How to Avoid Affairs

No matter how happily a woman may be married, it always pleases her to discover that there is a nice man who wishes she were not.

—H. L. MENCKEN

I see it as the problem we all have, of choosing a road in life. If I go into this work, or share my life with this person, then I cannot go down another road doing other work or sharing my life with another person. So it seems that no matter what choice I make, there is the loss of the road not taken.

—JOHN DUNNE

To be very frank for a moment, the extramatrimonial love affair has never struck me as so much an offense against religion, or a violation of what "the new morality" calls "sex taboos," as a breach of that loyalty and good faith that one partner expects of another under every other contract.

—CHANNING POLLOCK

Variability is one of the virtues of a woman. It avoids the crude requirement of polygamy. So long as you have one good wife you are sure to have a spiritual harem.

—G. K. CHESTERTON

Why an Affair Can
Be Tempting

We must now deal with one of the great enemies of a lasting relationship, sexual infidelity. And eventually we must deal with an apparent contradiction. In this book I have been arguing for both ecstasy and monogamy, which are, according to some, mutually exclusive. If one puts a premium on passion and believes in following the promptings of the heart, sooner or later the heart is liable to lead to someone new.

The Statistics on Infidelity

In fact, American people are turning to new partners with increasing frequency. The figures are startling. When several thousand men were asked, about half said they had extramarital affairs, and two-thirds said they would under certain circumstances. Adultery is clearly on the rise among women as well. According to one study, fully 26 percent of married women have extramarital sex by age twenty-five.[79]

The Legitimizing of Extramarital Sex

To some, these statistics merely confirm that singular love is unrealistic in this age of sexual freedom. There have always been those who have sought to legitimate adultery and who have tried to say that much good can come from a sexual fling. Swingers' clubs have sprung up on both coasts ("leave it to Americans to organize adultery," says William Kilpatrick), and many psychologists and marriage counselors tell us that an occasional affair can be salutary.

It is only one step beyond that to the new-time religion of a writer such as Ronald Mazur, a Unitarian minister. In his book, *The New Intimacy: Open-Ended Marriage and Alternative Life Styles*, Mazur announces that "traditional monogamy, with its rigid requirements for exclusive devotion and affection, even though hallowed by the theological concept of fidelity," is "a culturally approved mass neurosis."[80]

The Instinct for Fidelity

What Mazur calls a "mass neurosis"—our instinct to pair off and to desire exclusivity in the relationship—has very deep roots in almost every society, despite the efforts of some to regard it as quaint.

Every attempt to stamp out romantic attachment has failed. A monogamy-hating Yankee by the name of John Humphrey Noyes tried in 1848 when he founded the Oneida Community. Everything was shared in common, including coitus. The young and inexperienced were matched with older people, often in rooms set aside for what were euphemistically called "social purposes." When a couple began falling in love and a romantic attachment started to develop, the force of the community was mobilized to prevent it, for Noyes regarded monogamous love as "exclusive and selfish."

The experiment failed, of course, because people have a way of forming bonds, no matter what others do to prevent it. We are apparently constructed for more than casual sex.

Hence the Bible's clear-cut proscriptions against extramarital sex, and the long historical line of church support for monogamous marriage. The Scriptures take an unequivocal position. One need not take into account some "situational ethic" before making a decision as to whether to have an affair. It is always wrong. It may not be the worst of sins (for interesting reasons we usually think of sexual sins as more heinous than others), but it is a sin.

Chafing under such rules, it is easy for us to wonder if God decides to give us such commandments by fiat, simply to make us miserable. But in fact, God gives us such rules to make us happy. That is, having made us, He is in the best position to know how life will be the happiest for us. And the One who made us says that we will function best when we pledge ourselves to a mate and then remain faithful to the one we have chosen.

It is a popular canard that one can have a moderate amount of outside sex without harming one's marriage. Just be sure you keep it casual and be sure that you and your mate have an "honest understanding," the advisors say.

Most of the people with whom I work did not intend to leave their marriages when they reached for a little flirtation and sexual excitement. Let's take a fairly common scenario. Lila and Harold seem to have everything. He is a rising attorney; she has established a small retail shop, which is flourishing despite the fact that she took off time to have a new baby, with whom they both are smitten.

Lila finds herself going through a strange period, which she says she has been calling, for the lack of a better term, "an identity crisis." Harold is involved in a very complicated but potentially successful case that takes him out of town. They are not having much sex. She attributes this to the slowness with which her body is rebounding, and stops at a gym on the way home from work almost every evening. When he's home, he's sleepy, and she is bored. For the first time in her life, she feels unattractive.

A customer in her shop is a good-looking man, and almost without thinking about it, she tumbles into bed with him. Two weeks later and three sexual episodes later, she is in my office. The marriage sounds solid to me, and I am certain that I can persuade her to stop her affair before it gets out of hand. But she is not as pliable on this point as I had hoped. This is a wonderful new world, she explains, and surely she and Harold can work this out. They are both liberated and reasonable people, and she's going to tell Harold and give him permission to do the same thing.

In the ensuing months, I do not meet Harold, but knowing him through Lila's eyes I both sympathize with him and admire him. When at first he learns of her infidelity, he does not rage or walk out. He is remarkably introspective and apologetic. He feels that this has happened because he has been neglecting his wife. He is much more amorous and changes his traveling schedule to be at home with her and to take care of the baby more.

He wants her to give up her lover. She does for two weeks, but one lonely day when things have gone wrong at the shop, she calls him and the affair is resumed. She and

Harold talk more about having an "open marriage." The next time Lila is in, she is almost euphoric. Harold stayed out all night, and she thinks he has a girlfriend. Now her guilt is assuaged, and she feels that they are on their way to having the best of both worlds.

It is several months later that she comes in. This time she is anything but euphoric. She looks haggard, her hair is shapeless, there is none of the old vitality in her.

Harold wants a divorce. What has happened? He has fallen in love with his new friend of course. And what about her own affair? She still sees him, but he seems strangely distant now that she's no longer the challenge she once was. And the baby? That child will forever carry some of the anguish of two people who supposed that they could ignore the accumulated wisdom of many centuries.

For all our so-called sophisticated and permissive society, affairs continue to break up good, functional marriages, damaging children, breaking dreams, and causing permanent damage to people who did nothing to invite injury. In my office, I see these refugees. Children who did their best, who tried to make the right choices. But, because of parents to whom they happened to be born, or because of the mates to whom they happened to be married, they find their lives bombed out. They were not combatants, they did not ask for the artillery; they only happened to be a part of a family in which someone planted an explosive.

Can You Feel Love Toward More Than One?

In looking at the complex reasons that we are tempted to stray, we must first dispel two misconceptions about the phenomenon of extramarital affairs. There is, for instance, the mistaken idea that you can have feelings of love for only one person at a time and that if you feel that you are falling in love with someone new, you must have fallen out of love with your mate. That is nonsense. I talk to people almost every day who say that they are occasionally obsessed with thoughts about some new person, but that they still have tender and loving feelings for their partners.

There is another canard one often hears on this topic: "She never would have strayed unless there was something wrong with her marriage." Wrong again. A large survey of women's sexual attitudes asked those women who were having outside sex how they rated their marriages: 61 percent rated their overall relationship with their husbands as "good" or "very good."[81]

Biologically We Are Indiscriminate

What is it, then, that they want? If the marriage is happy and the sex is fine, why would one partner go to the trouble (and usually it *is* trouble) of burrowing into a secret life?

Because of animal desire, for one thing. One of the curious contradictions we carry with us is that, while we have a mental instinct to be monogamous, biologically we are capable of being attracted to almost any one of the opposite sex. God made us that way, doubtless for the propagation of the species. It is a foundational drive in all species—the organism is determined to propagate itself. In the animal kingdom, this instinct to propagate overrules many other impulses, and this ability to copulate with more than one person is quite strong.

When You Are Most Vulnerable

At certain periods in one's life, the stresses of circumstances increase one's vulnerability to an extramarital fling. They are usually those points when one is feeling discouraged or especially needing affection. If the stress happens to occur at a time when the marriage is not going well, the danger is intensified. Dr. Avodah Offit, in her book *Night Thoughts: Reflections of a Sex Therapist,* suggests over a dozen predictable times when sexual infidelity is more likely to occur, and all have to do with loss or stress. Family crises, for instance, are highly unsettling to one's routine and sense of security and make one vulnerable:

- Pregnancy and childbirth
- The period during which small children receive a great deal of attention at home
- A child's accident or a mate's illness
- Times of bereavement

Offit goes on to point out other situations that are unsettling and make it easier to turn to a new sexual experience for solace. They include any point when a woman or a man is

- Changing jobs
- Deciding on or beginning a new career
- Heavily involved in expansion or success
- Traveling extensively
- Depressed by failure
- Watching the children leave for college[82]

The Lure of the Forbidden

Another element thickens the plot and makes it a little more difficult to be true for a lifetime: we are all a little fascinated with the forbidden. Denis de Rougemont, in his classic study, *Love in the Western World,* goes so far as to say that it is the nature of romantic love to be profane. De Rougemont thinks that romance was an invention of the twelfth-century troubadour poets, who indeed were more interested in depicting the intrigue and machinations of adultery than in describing the monotony of married love.[83] I do not intend to espouse here de Rougemont's version of the history of love, let alone his thesis that romance is adulterous by nature. However, there is a certain amount of truth in his point that love thrives on obstacles. The protests of Romeo and Juliet's parents intensified their children's passion, and the forbiddenness of Guinevere's love for Launcelot made it more interesting. Take away the impediments, and it loses some excitement. If Dr. Zhivago had married Lara first, he doubtless would have desired Tonia later. The grass always looks greener on the other side of the fence.

The Need to Be Needed

I worked with a woman once who had been having sex regularly with a man across the street for more than three years before her husband found out. "I'm still not sure why I did it," she said. "I know this is no excuse, but what I was really looking for was to be needed and to be desired. Dennis is a good husband, and anytime I'd ask him, he'd say, 'Of *course* I love you.' And I don't doubt that he does, but it was as if he could take me or leave me. So when this guy started coming over in the afternoons and wrote me poems and seemed to find me so attractive and irresistable, I gave in.

"I read once that Ann Landers says that men give love to get sex, and women give sex to get love. That was probably what happened in my case. The sex was almost incidental. What I seemed to crave was to be desired."

It is a universal longing, and it is a longing that often gets thwarted in long-term traditional marriages. Not only do you find your partner's body less exciting after making love thousands of times and in every position, but your partner is also less interested in you. And the latter hurts more than the former.

Boredom

The last and perhaps the most common cause for slipping is boredom. No long-standing relationship can compete in excitement with a brand-new affair. A vivacious young woman in her second marriage said to me, "I have everything. There is no reason for me to be unhappy, but I'm bored with my marriage and have this crazy infatuation for a man at church. What's wrong with me?"

There's probably nothing wrong with her. She is being smitten with an impulse that comes to many people who are in the doldrums, an impulse that almost everyone who has loved one person for any length of time has had to wrestle down. I believe that the lure of the affair lies not so much in the nature of romance as in the nature of boredom and that there are specific things one can do to control wandering erotic feelings. Or to repair the breach if such a mistake has already occurred.

Suggestions for Keeping Yourself True

Given our sexual natures and given the bombardment of sexual stimuli with which our culture furnishes us, it is important to have a strategy for being faithful to the one you love. Here are some suggestions:

1. *Decide what you believe.* The sooner you can make up your mind what you really believe about sexual commitment, the better it will be, because in the long run what you do about having an affair will depend more on your beliefs than on your feelings. The Bible urges fidelity. We

are to be true to the mates we have chosen through thick and thin, through periods of sexual excitement and through periods when the excitement is missing.

If you do not accept that position, as many do not, your behavior will be the natural consequence of what you have decided about monogamy. Your actions will have been thought out beforehand and will be in accord with your beliefs. The persons most to be pitied are those who mush along in our sexual wilderness, uncertain as to what kind of sexual life they want, waiting to adapt their behavior to whatever opportunities come along. Such people wake up the next morning with the too-late realization that they have jeopardized their most precious possessions—their families—without thinking through the consequences.

2. *Decide whether you are bored with your mate or with yourself.* If many affairs begin out of boredom, as I suggested earlier, it is important to determine whether your mate has really become uninteresting or whether you are bored with yourself and your life. If the answer is the latter, get busy making some changes. Almost any change. Perhaps you should think about a new career for the second half of your life or take up skydiving or sculpting. If your basic ennui is with life itself, a new sexual partner will not help except for the short run. New, exciting partners have a way of becoming old, boring partners if the real problem is yourself.

3. *Regulate your fantasy life.* I once knew a famous religious figure who was caught in a sexual scandal, and everyone was shocked that this man could slip so badly. But a mutual friend who knew him well said that he was not at all surprised that it happened, and in fact expected it. I asked why he'd predicted such a thing? "Because I saw what he read," my friend replied. "I know what sort of magazines he bought at the airport when he left on a trip and the sort of

movies he watched. It was inevitable that he would eventually act out those fantasies."

When Jesus tells us that if we lust after a woman we have already committed adultery with her, surely he is not saying that we are guilty of sin every time we have a sexual thought about someone outside our marriage. If so, many of us sin grievously every day. Rather, I think he was saying that anyone who fantasizes at length about extramarital sex is eventually going to live out the fantasy. He is simply saying that the thought is father of the deed, and if you think about any sin long enough, you may as well regard yourself as having committed it already, for you are certain to do so.

The computer people have a saying about their machines: "Garbage in, garbage out." The same truism applies to the mind. If you continue to fill it with trash novels and pornography, sooner or later your morals will break down under that constant bombardment. A few years ago, someone examined one of the popular soap operas, *General Hospital,* and reported that the seventeen major characters were involved in four divorces, two premarital pregnancies, two drug addictions, and four illicit affairs.[84] None of us can withstand an unlimited exposure to salacious material without having it influence our behavior.

4. *Learn your limits.* Some people say that, because there is always the possibility of sexual attraction, one should restrict friends to those of the same sex. But impoverishing your life impoverishes your marriage. I have some wonderful women friends, and knowing them helps me understand and love my wife better. Diane and I have an agreement. We are free to make friends with anyone we want and to have lunch anywhere with anyone. No permission necessary. But we both know our sexual limits and if we think

we are beginning to reach those limits, we bail out in a hurry. No friendship is so important that we will jeopardize our marriage.

5. *Remember that the little decisions are the important ones.* Richard DeVoss, one of the founders of Amway, talks about his rise in the business world. He started from scratch to become co-owner of a company that grosses more than $1 billion a year. "It's amazing," he says, "how much of our lives is determined not by big decisions, but by little ones that pile up on us."[85] When their company was just beginning, and the two men working in their basements would be tired and not sure they could work any longer, they had to decide whether to quit that night or work another half hour. Those were the crucial decisions, which, added up, made the difference between failure and success.

This is a valuable principle to get hold of and it works for success in relationships as much as in business. That is, the real test is not the question "Shall I take off my clothes and have an affair with this woman?" By that time, it's already too late. The crucial questions are the little ones earlier, such as "Shall I pick up the phone and call her?" or "Would it hurt if I sent her just this one card saying that I love her and would *like* to go to bed with her even though we've both agreed we won't?"

Those are the crucial intersections at which our destinies are determined. So Suggestion Number Five is: Win the battle by winning the little skirmishes.

6. *Remember that sex is not everything.* As surprising as it may be to some of the readers of "Penthouse Forum," there are some people living on this globe, and quite contentedly at that, who have gone several years without sexual intercourse. I am not recommending celibacy as a way of life but I am suggesting that sex is not all there is. Other expe-

riences, such as the experience of kindness, can sometimes cause almost as much joy.

I know a woman whose husband had some complicated surgery almost a decade ago that incapacitated him for any customary sexual intercourse. When the extent of his surgery was explained to him the next day, he was devastated, and rehearsed a little speech for his wife about how he would understand if she decided to get a divorce. She knew him so well that when he started to tell her she knew where the speech was going and cut him off with a snort: "Sam, if you're going to get rid of me, you'll have to think up a lot better excuse than this one." Then she turned tender and said she'd rather live her life with half of him than with all of any other man. And, as nearly as I can tell, she is a fulfilled woman.

When a girl marries, she exchanges the attention of all other men she knew for the inattention of one.

—HELEN ROWLAND

Lord, when we are wrong, make us willing to change, and when we are right, make us easy to live with.

—PETER MARSHALL

Marriage must incessantly contend with a monster which devours everything, that is, familiarity.

—HONORÉ DE BALZAC

"Woman, where are they? Has no one condemned You?" She said, "No one, Lord." And Jesus said, "Neither do I condemn you; go and do not sin again."

—JOHN 8:10–11

Alternatives to Jealousy

If no marriage is immune to the problems and the situations that lead to extramarital sex, we need to look at ways to prevent it from happening in our marriages—and what to do to keep an affair from wrecking our lives if it does happen.

Does Jealousy Hurt or Hinder?

Today, it is widely regarded as poor form to express jealousy. And there is a certain amount of validity to this warning. If you are the jealous type, it is advisable to examine your jealousy to see if it is pathological. The woman who hisses every time her husband looks at a pretty girl on the sidewalk or touches a female friend at a party is not helping the relationship. What she needs to examine is the reason for her unreasonable anger. Either it is an attempt to keep her husband on a very tight rope, which is not very smart. Or it is a case of being insecure: she is really asking for more love from her husband. She has a perfect right to ask for more affection if she is weathering a storm of self-doubt, but her indirect way of angling for it is counterproductive. Her jealous outbursts are accusatory and are quite likely to start a fight.

Having said that, I must now say that in moderate amounts jealousy is a sign of love. Somewhere people got the idea that the way to hang on to our mates these days is to stay cool and act as if we don't care whether our partners fall for other people. The nonpossessive, liberated ideal.

But indifference never aroused love in anyone. Diane and I were once watching a television program about straying husbands; wives were being interviewed about what they would do if they learned that their husbands were philandering. My ordinarily easygoing wife turned to me and said, "I know what I'd do: I'd fight for you!" I do not plan to test her on that, but I was flattered to the core that she loves me that much. And every man I know feels the same way. So, to the extent that jealousy is an expression of love, it may not be all bad.

Suggestions for Hanging on to Your Mate

But there are more constructive things one can do to ensure against infidelity. Here are some suggestions:

1. *Step up your sex life.* A fascinating pattern emerges when a woman learns that her husband is seeing another woman. There are usually tears and lots of anger and hostility, of course, but in 99 percent of the cases there also is an increase in their sex life. When I saw that pattern in the first few couples, I was amazed at the wife's reaction. I

would have supposed that if he was sleeping with some other woman she would be so incensed that her earliest weapon would be to deny him sex. She would give him an ultimatum that he could not make love to her so long as he was seeing her competitor. Or she would feel so rejected that she would not have sex for fear that he would compare them.

As I say, that would have been the behavior I expected. But after working with hundreds of couples in this trauma, I now know that in nearly every instance her reaction will be the opposite: she finds herself sexually excited, cuts loose with abandon, and becomes much more aggressive in bed. A few months later, a delayed reaction frequently occurs, when she becomes unresponsive, but during this early crisis she is highly aroused. Why? Simple. She instinctively knows that's how to get her man back. She's not designing nor is she faking feelings in order to manipulate him. The sex drive is a curious thing; it responds to very deep psychic changes, and without her consciously thinking that she should become more sexual in order to get her man back, her sexuality suddenly comes to the rescue and she finds herself alive and fiery in bed.

I make that point in order to make another: if you have that much ability to increase your sexual interaction in order to get your mate *back*, why not do it in order to prevent an affair?

2. *Talk to your mate about how you would feel if it happened.* Like sex in general, the possibility of an affair is on everyone's mind, yet it is a topic that few couples—even close couples—ever discuss with each other. They often talk it over with their friends, speculating about the possibility, wondering what would happen. But not with their mates. If it is important to you that your partner try to be true,

then say so. Make clear that you would be very, very hurt.

Do *not* say, "If you ever mess around, I don't want to know about it." That is an invitation to your partner to try to get away with something and gives the impression that messing around might be OK so long as it's kept quiet. Understandably, we may want to be left ignorant, and perhaps we should be, but it's not a smart thing to say.

I suggest that you tell your mate how much it means to you that he or she be faithful, and then don't make any predictions about your behavior in the event that you discover adultery. People will sometimes make threats, such as "If you ever cheat, once is all it will take, and I'll be out the door." But that is not a smart thing to say either. None of us can predict what our behavior will be.

3. *The best deterrent of all is to make clear your own commitment.* It doesn't hurt to tell your lover (without going into detail) that you have had some opportunities to be unfaithful and that you've been true, if in fact that has been the case.

You are walking a fine line here. If you happen to be fighting off several men at your office, it doesn't make your husband very secure to hear the lurid details. On the other hand, if you *are* being true and if sexual fidelity continues to be an important tenet in your pact, it doesn't hurt at all to say that. Some people have been married so long that they assume that their mate knows how loyal they are. But too many assumptions are always dangerous. Successfully married couples continue to feed each other data about their feelings. They explain which feelings have changed, and if there are others that have *not* changed (such as their position on adultery), they say that also.

4. *Avoid prolonged absences.* Whoever said that absence makes the heart grow fonder had no idea what he was saying. Many

adolescent love affairs end when the girl goes away to college and the boy stays home. And the two-career families with a husband working in Seattle and a wife in Denver are playing with dynamite.

It is true, of course, that a brief absence makes one's feelings for the beloved more intense. "I miss you desperately," Diane will write to me when I'm off speaking at some convention. Our pattern of living a shared life has been interrupted, and being apart poignantly makes me realize what I'm missing. But I wouldn't dare stay away from her for, say, six weeks. She might get accustomed to living without me. The romantic idealist will say, "You must not have a very secure love if you would stop missing each other that soon." What the romantic overlooks is the structure of the organism to compensate for losses. It can tolerate only so much pain, and quickly readjusts. And I don't ever plan to stay away long enough that my wife's pain begins to wane.

Many women who look for other men while their husbands are working overtime are actually looking for conversation more than caresses. As psychiatrist David Reuben says, "After wrestling with children, housework, shopping, dogs and cats, door-to-door salesmen and leaking washing machines from 7 A.M. to dark—and eating a solitary dinner—she begins to suffer from chronic emotional malnutrition."[86] An ounce of prevention on the part of a husband at this juncture is worth a lot.

As Jack explains,

When I found out Ellen was going out with another man, I fell apart. Finally, I went to see our minister to ask him to take care of the kids after I left. I don't know how he did it, but he explained to me what was really going on. He said that Ellen's infidelity was really a desperate cry for help. He said she didn't want *another* man—she just wanted the man she married. That made sense to me—I was pushing so hard to get ahead that I hadn't been home one night out of ten for months. We're back together again now, and I'm giving her all of me she can stand. That was four years ago, and so far I haven't heard any complaints.[87]

5. *Use positive reinforcement.* An occasional compliment and a "thank you" will do more to modify your mate's behavior than any amount of threats or jealous nagging.

If you are married to an attractive person who is sure to get some come-ons from people at work, make it clear that you're aware of all that. Nothing will build up a man's ego more than to have his wife say when he leaves, "You're sure a sexy man. I'll bet those gals at the office drool over you, but tonight you're mine, and I'm going to attack that great body of yours when you come home."

Explain how much it means to you to be married to a lover who is true. Many of us are blessed with wives or husbands who have high standards and who love us enough to turn down some very strong inclinations. But how long has it been since we expressed our appreciation to them for resisting those opportunities?

6. *Trust your mate.* The surest way for a husband to send his wife into the arms of another lover is to accuse her constantly of having an affair. If you are uneasy, insecure, suspicious, and constantly questioning, you may think that you are helping to hold your mate in line, but usually it has the opposite effect. No one likes to be distrusted, especially when we are being true. And such accusations tend to bring out the worst in us. On the other hand, being trusted tends to bring out the best in us. It is a great gift if your wife believes in you, knows that you are a good person, and does not grill you about all your movements. And when your wife puts that sort of confidence in you, you will usually do everything in your power to live up to that image. "Call a dog by a good name," an old proverb

says, "and he will do everything he can to live up to that reputation."

When Your Mate Has an Affair

"I recently discovered that my husband is having an affair," said a young patient. "I thought we had a perfect marriage. We're such good friends, and he told me I was a terrific lover. I feel shattered. The woman he's seeing isn't even as pretty as I am!"

It is a devastating experience, and I always respond profoundly to such pain. With the high incidence of extramarital sex today, many people must face the fact that their partner has already been to bed with someone else. Here are some suggestions for dealing with it.

1. *Remember that it's not the end of the world.* An affair probably is not even the end of your marriage unless you want it to be. I know many wonderful marriages in which there has been such an earthquake in the past and in which the "wronged" partner is very glad that he or she did not panic unnecessarily.

The worst thing about discovering that you have been cuckolded is that you feel rejected and uncared for. You feel that you must not be attractive any longer or that your technique in bed must be rotten. But in fact it is possible that none of the above is true. Your partner may be very much in love with you, and the affair may have had little meaning. I have a friend who says, "Why do we make so much of the sexual act? Sex is an incident. If my wife went to bed with another man (as she did many years ago) I think I could handle it again. We have a lot together; I know she loves me and I love her, and I wouldn't let one incident like that ruin everything we have."

I'm not sure that I agree with him entirely, but it is true that sex sometimes can be a brief and relatively insignificant episode. When your wife has been on a business trip and you discover that she spent the night in her hotel room with another man, it is difficult to believe that it was without feeling or that your marriage is not in jeopardy. We tend to think the worst. Here is the contradiction: most of us, confiding in a friend or a therapist, feel that we could have a temporary fling without loving our mates any less and without wanting to end our marriages. But it is hard to give our partners the same benefit of the doubt.

2. *Do not stifle your emotions.* Of course you are going to feel hurt, and if you need to cry, for goodness' sake cry. Women come into my office on an emergency basis when they've just learned of an affair. They say, "I've got to get hold of myself. If I keep crying this way, I know I'm going to drive him away." Not so. If you hurt, express it. If you're angry, say so.

3. *But do not use the transgression as a club.* Some of us derive a certain satisfaction from being sinned against, in part because another's sin can make our own sins look less monstrous and can give us a weapon for controlling our partner.

In a wrenching scene in *Bachelorhood: Tales of the Metropolis,* Phillip Lopate tells of the night his father beat his mother because of her affair with a man named Willy. "We heard her through the door, each sob feeding involuntarily on the last, winding down bitterly to a questioning whimper, like that of a crying doll pushed forward at the waist."[88] After looking at such a picture, one turns desperately to the tender descriptions of Christ's compassion for the woman at the Sychar well or the woman caught in adultery. Our Lord was not a moral relativist: he lined out clear standards of right and wrong. At the same time, he knew that we live in an imperfect world and that the person who tries to live by high standards—and occasionally slips—is a notch above those who do not try.

A few pious critics have lately castigated Father Andrew Greeley for writing novels about lust, greed, and adultery, and about priests who are sometimes unsuccessful in keeping their vows of chastity. But Greeley is eloquent in his rationale, stated in "A Personal Afterword" to *Thy Brother's Wife*. The novel is, he says "a tale of commitments that are imperfectly made and imperfectly kept—but that are still kept," and of a God "who draws straight with crooked lines, who easily and quickly forgives, and who wants to love us with the tenderness of a mother."[89]

When we have been wounded by another's mistake, it may not be possible to be as forgiving as God, but that is our ideal. And at a minimum, the Christian will vow not to use the failures of others as a club with which to beat them farther into the ground.

4. *Analyze the circumstances.* In one survey, when asked whether they would leave their husbands if they discovered an affair, women answered as follows:

- Nine percent said they would ignore the evidence.
- Ten percent said they would file for divorce.
- Seventy percent said it would depend. They would try to find out why the affair took place before making a judgment.[90]

The last response is wise, because the circumstances of the event can differ enormously. For instance, it may make a difference whether your mate sought out the sex or was seduced. You may have trouble getting data on that, but we have all known situations where a good person is subjected to a carefully planned campaign. And if that onslaught happens to coincide with a vulnerable moment, few of us could be sure that we would survive.

When I was younger, I'm afraid I took a rather harsh

and condescending view of those who had committed adultery. But as Goethe somewhere says, one need only grow older to become more gentle in one's judgments. I can see no fault in others that I might not have committed myself.

5. *Try to assess your own responsibility.* Most people to whom I talk who have any humility in them at all say, "I've got to take part of the blame. I was making lots of mistakes." If you talk such questions over with your mate, a potentially dangerous event might bring you closer together.

6. *Don't inquire about the lurid details.* There is a macabre impulse in some of us to ask, when wronged, for every minute aspect of the wrongdoing. I'm not sure I fully understand this impulse. Sometimes it looks like self-torture. But more often, I think, it is a malicious impulse. Making your partner recount all the conversations, all the sexual acts, all the emotions exchanged, keeps your partner in an inferior position. Asking him or her to confess the painful events all over and to sit helplessly by when you go through all the hurt again is severe punishment for both parties.

7. *Whatever happens, do not try to retaliate in kind.* That, of course, is the natural instinct: to give your mate some of the same medicine and to have an affair yourself. Sometimes you are not seeking revenge, but desperately wanting to prove to yourself or to your partner that you are still desirable. The instinct is understandable, but the results are often disastrous. I haven't kept records, but I think I know of more divorces that have occurred when a second partner has a retaliatory affair than when the initial slip occurred. An already shaky situation can be destroyed by such an impulse.

8. *In choosing whether to leave your mate, ask whether the infidelity was a slip from the norm or an irreversible pattern.* Some

men and women will never be faithful to their mates because deep down they do not plan to do so. We all have known people—usually women—who have put up with a wandering spouse year after year. If you are able to do that, and if it turns out to be beneficial for you or your children, more power to you. But you need to know that you do not have to. The Bible urges that you be long-suffering, but it gives you plenty of room to bail out if you're married to a sexual junkie.

9. *Do not allow your self-image to be destroyed.* Some people who have cheating mates feel that it is axiomatic that they themselves must have something wrong with them. Women may feel that if they couldn't keep their husbands at home, they themselves must be unlovable. Let's put the worst possible interpretation on the matter: assume that your husband is in love with the other woman, that he doesn't love you anymore, and that he says you have been a rotten wife. You can't expect to come out of that unruffled, but the fact that one man has deserted you for someone else does not necessarily mean that you are unattractive or unlovable. And the fact that he says you have been a rotten wife does not necessarily make it so.

I talked this week to a wonderful woman with three children. She stopped by our office to tell us about her new boyfriend and her upcoming marriage. "He's wonderful," she said. "He even opens doors for me and walks on the street side of the sidewalk. I feel like a teenager in love all over again." That was good to hear, because we spent countless hours with her during a much more tragic time. Her child had been seriously ill, she became run down physically, and she began drinking heavily. Her husband's response was to quit his job and move in with a neighbor woman up the street. As we sat together back then and she sobbed hour after hour, I wondered if I could survive if I were in her shoes. But one of the therapists in our office knew how to love her back to health and help her recover her sense of worth.

It was wonderful to have her drop in, later, and to see the change.

We don't always have such dramatic successes, but such recoveries show that it need not be the end of your self-respect if you have lost a round in the highly competitive game of love and sex.

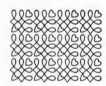

PART VI

Guidelines for Building a Lasting Relationship

The main fact of life for me is love or its absence. Whether life is worth living depends on whether there is love in life.

—R. D. LAING

Love means to commit oneself without guarantee, to give oneself completely in the hope that our love will produce love in the loved person. Love is an act of faith, and whoever is of little faith is of little love.

—ERICH FROMM

Love does not consist in gazing at each other but in looking outward together in the same direction.

—ANTOINE DE SAINT-EXUPERY

Love alters not with his brief hours and weeks,
But bears it out even to the edge of doom.
    If this be error and upon me proved,
    I never writ, nor no man ever loved.

—SHAKESPEARE

Love as Choice

Is constancy possible in our fluid world? Is it feasible to pledge fidelity to one person and to promise to love that one until death? It is impossible to answer such questions without looking at Kierkegaard's view of love as an act of the will. Love, Kierkegaard concluded, is not a feeling but a choice.

Kierkegaard's analysis, in turn, was an explication of that single sentence from Christ's teaching that has bobbed up in our discussion in many contexts: "You shall love your neighbor as yourself." Kierkegaard's point about Christ's command is that it was just that—a command.[91] He found that startling, because most people assume that love is a feeling and we can't help how we feel.

Then why would Jesus command us to love? Kierkegaard's conclusion was that love is evidently far more than an emotion, and he doubtless is correct. He probably overstates the case in averring that it is a choice rather than a feeling, because, more precisely, love is a mixture of both. The more I talk to patients who are successful in their love relationships over any length of time, I realize how much their love depends on will. It is something they *do* as well as something they feel. At times the tenderness and joy and affection predominate, and at other times those feelings are absent. Unless one is going to flit from one new partner to another, love must have a consistency that is thicker than emotion. It must be comprised of a healthy amount of will.

Benjamin Disraeli, the great British statesman, flitted from one partner to another for fifteen years. At twenty-one he began an affair with Mrs. Sarah Austen, who was the wife of a family friend and who persuaded her husband to lend Disraeli large sums of money. Later, he got a new mistress, Mrs. Clara Bolton, a party-giving doctor's wife, to help him with literary and political connections. But within a year, he had exchanged her for the oversexed and dazzling Lady Henrietta Stykes, a mother of four.

With such an unsavory reputation, when Disraeli proposed marriage to Mary Anne Evans, a rich widow twelve years older than him, no one, including the woman, thought he was marrying her for love. In fact, he made no pretense of loving her at first. He was marrying her because she had a house in fashionable Park Lane and an income of 4,000 pounds a year. She was neither beautiful nor brilliant. She wore outrageous costumes that defied the current fashion, and she never pretended to have her husband's intellect. She said that she "could never remember which came first, the Greeks or the Romans."

This relationship, which seemed to have so little prospect for success, turned out to be one of the finest marriages in England. Home, to Disraeli's increasing delight, became a place where he could ease into his mental slippers and bask in the warmth of Mary Anne's adoration. Every night he hurried home from the House of Commons to tell her the day's news. No matter how silly or scatterbrained she might appear, he never criticized her and sprang to her defense with ferocious loyalty. When he was created Lord Beaconsfield, he rushed home, threw his arms around her, and said, "My love, you are now Lady Beaconsfield."

Gone forever, so far as we know, were his profligate ways. "She is more a mistress than a wife," he said. And after thirty years of marriage she said, "My life has been simply one long scene of happiness, thanks to his kindness." She was, according to Dale Carnegie, a genius at the most important thing for women in marriage: the art of handling men. She simply did not believe he could fail, and she spent the rest of her lifetime talking about her husband, praising him and admiring him. The result? "We have been married thirty years," Disraeli said, "and I have never been bored by her." (Yet some people thought because Mary Anne didn't know history she must be stupid!)

They had a little joke between them. "You know," Disraeli would say, "I only married you for your money." And Mary Anne, smiling, would reply, "Yes, but if you had it to do over again, you'd marry me for love, wouldn't you?"

And he admitted it was true. And so, his life now focused by his marriage and his career inspired by his wife's love, Disraeli went on to become Prime Minister of England twice, and to become one of the greatest statesmen of all time.

But their love was not merely based on some weak-at-the-knees feeling of being in love. Their love was commitment, and out of that fidelity the emotions grew.[92]

The Growth of Love

C. S. Lewis advocates love as an act of the will. Do not waste time wondering whether you "love" another, he suggests, *act* as if you do. "As soon as we do this, we find one of the great secrets. When you are behaving as if you loved someone, you will presently come to love him." Lewis goes on to explain that the process works equally in reverse: "If you injure someone you dislike, you will find yourself disliking him more. If you do him a good turn, you will find yourself disliking him less."[93]

The reader might well protest at this juncture that I have throughout this book been promoting the joy of passionate and ecstatic love, and now I am saying that feelings are unimportant, that love is a matter of commitment and exercise of the will. But I am not saying that at all. What I am saying is that your feelings will come and go, and that commitment will give your relationship the momentum to carry you through the rough places.

The Fluid Self

This instinct to pledge yourself to be true to your mate is considerably different from the current passion to "experience everything," to "flow with your feelings," and to "live for the present."

Much of the present-day psychology provides no basis for lasting relationships. It proclaims, rather, a self that exists as a free-floating, unencumbered entity. We are being encouraged to find the real meaning of life in self-actualization rather than in commitment to others.

Advocates of this approach say the trick is to stay "fluid." If the relationship you are in becomes sluggish, move out of it. And you shouldn't feel guilty, because lasting and exclusive relationships are not very practical anyhow. We are all in the process of changing from the person we once were to someone else.

But the worship of the spontaneous and the fluid leaves a great deal to be desired. Many people I know fall in and out of love a lot, but their feelings, although intense, tend not to be very profound.

Love as Loyalty

A woman of seventy-six came to my office to tell me how terrible her marriage had become. "I married him for better or for worse," she said, "but I didn't know it would get *this* much worse."

Her husband had been retired a few years when one night he couldn't sleep and went from one room to another babbling. Senility does not usually set in so suddenly, but her husband's personality changed overnight. He had always been quiet and temperate and mild-mannered, but now he swore, smoked and drank to excess, and followed her around all day long. Even while she was talking to me, he was pacing in our outer office.

I inquired about helping him, and she told of all the doctors she had taken him to. The only solution they could offer was to put him in an institution. She was near the breaking point, it seemed to me. I felt that I should give her permission to do something about this deranged man with whom she lived—to put him away or, if that was not possible, to divorce him.

But when I began to talk about those possibilities, her eyes acquired fire, and I realized quickly that this woman was not here to get my permission or advice on what she should do. She knew full well what she wanted to do—she wanted to be able to go back home and give some more tenderness and love to her sick husband. She had come to my office to ventilate some of her displeasure, and it gave her a little relief. With an almost visible sigh, she then readied herself to go back and give it her best again.

When she left, I sat in my chair a long while pondering how much more depth there was to her love than to the starry-eyed feelings of those who flit from one titillating experience to another. This woman did not have any tingling sensations about her husband just now. Her overpowering emotion was that she'd like to wring his neck. She was more revolted by his present personality than attracted by it. Nevertheless, he had been good to her for decades and had worked all their married life to provide good things for her, and now that he was sick and disagreeable and followed her around like a puppy, she was still as committed to him as when she was "in love" with him.

The Choice to Endure

I might just as well say it now, because it needs to be said at some juncture in this discussion of the deeper meanings of love: if you choose to love for a lifetime, you will be choosing, in some measure, to suffer. To sacrifice.

One of the most important things about Jesus was that he was "a man of sorrows and acquainted with grief," because sorrow and grief await us in our relationships sooner or later. In fact, he elevated suffering to a virtue. He could have chosen the pursuit of pleasure, or the development of the "fluid self" so admired by the psychologists of our day. But instead he elected to value the happiness of others as a higher good than his own pleasure, and thus he brought us redemption.

Without overdramatizing the effect of a lasting, committed love to our beloved ones, we can, to some lesser degree, be such agents of redemption. I think of Carl Rogers's wife Helen, for instance. When Rogers was in his forties, he went through a period of more than a year when he had no sex drive whatever. Not toward his wife or toward anyone. No medical cause was found. "But my wife Helen," he wrote later, "was confident that my normal urges would return and simply 'stood with me' in my predicament. Her quiet, continuing love meant a great deal to me and probably was the best therapy I could have had."[94] Such commitment is redemptive.

I do not know any way one can stay happily married and raise children to adulthood without some willingness to suffer. One does not build a warm and loving family by seeking personal pleasure as the end-all and be-all of life. There are occasions when you must endure. To use the Apostle Paul's words, "Love bears all things, believes all things, hopes all things, endures all things."

If a woman feels very attracted to a sympathetic man who happens to be her husband's best friend, and if the attraction happens to occur when her husband is overweight and depressed about his career, to be true to her marriage vows at that moment is going to require some suffering. Similarly, when your children go to college and to help pay the bills you have to drive an old clunker of a car for three years, you suffer a little.

No one is pretending the soul-stirring ecstasy of early romance can ever be constant in a marriage. If your relationship is based on that, you will not be together long. But if your relationship is based on the trust of your pledge, on your joint determination to stay together because you believe in the family, the joys will return in waves. When Harry Truman was an old, retired politician, one would not have expected any sentimental nonsense from his lips. But he said of his wife Bess, "We went to Sunday school, public school from the fifth grade through high school, graduated in the same class and marched down life's road together. For me she still has the blue eyes and the golden hair of yesteryear."[95]

As couples continue to make their way to church altars and make promises to cherish one another "in sickness and in health, in plenty and in want," the phrases may sound old and antiquated to the liberated woman and the urbane man-about-town who are only interested in taking care of themselves. But anyone with any sense of history knows that there will be times when those liberated and urbane people will be sick. Sometime they will need someone who loves them not because he or she is attractive but because they are committed to one another.

Many years ago, when I was a pastor, my telephone rang early one morning. The man on the other end apologized for calling so early, but told me that his wife, who was in the hospital, had been asking for me during the night. He wondered if I could drop by during the morning. I dressed hurriedly and went immediately, because it was my cherished friend, David Leek, and I knew that, diffident as he was by nature, if he called, it was urgent. Betty had been dying of cancer for most of the four years I had known those two people. They were romantics at heart, and I had witnessed their tender affection for each other in dozens of ways. He had wooed and won her twenty-eight years before, beating out several handsome competitors on their college campus, and it had been a wonderful match.

When I arrived at the hospital, she had lapsed back into a coma. But David was still there, with his chair pulled up close to hers, making sure that her days and nights were

spent with as much comfort as possible. That nothing un-
seemly happened to her body.

Later, as I drove away, thinking about that couple in the
hospital room, I realized how much deeper their love was
than some ephemeral emotion. They lent dignity to each
other. He still had his suit and tie on from his work the
day before. I marveled at the reserves that are called out in
some people when a loved one is in trouble. What sustains
them? What enables such a man to sit in a hospital, still
dressed in his suit, all night long? What is it that makes a
woman wait for her prisoner-of-war husband month after
month? What is it that makes a wife visit her husband in
the penitentiary every Sunday, year in and year out?

It is something more than ecstatic love. Something more
than a romantic interlude, surely. It has to do with perse-
verence, loyalty, and commitment. Sometimes you do those
things not because you are overcome with passion, but because you are committed. That is, you believe in honoring
your word. You do not walk away from your obligations
simply because the pleasure is missing.

If I had to choose between ecstatic love and commitment
love, I would choose the latter. And if the occasion ever
calls for it, I aspire to be the sort of lover I saw there beside
a dying woman's bed.

Even if marriages are made in heaven, man has to be responsible for the maintenance.

—JOHN GRAHAM

In marriage reverence is more important even than love. . . . a steady awareness in each that the other has a kinship with the eternal.

—F. J. SHIELD

Love is . . . not a result; it is a cause. . . . People talk about love as though it were something you could give, like an armful of flowers. . . . Love is a force *in you* that enables you to give *other* things. . . . It is a power, like money, or steam or electricity. It is valueless unless you can give something else *by means* of it.

—ANNE MORROW LINDBERGH

The older you get the more you realize that kindness is synonymous with happiness.

—LIONEL BARRYMORE

Kindness: The Neglected Virtue

Family therapists like myself are forever being asked the same question on talk shows: "Dr. McGinnis, to what do you attribute the breakup of so many marriages today? Is it sexual problems? Money difficulties? Is it because families watch television instead of talking?

In my experience, none of those is a *cause;* they are merely symptoms. The real cause is so simple and so obvious that I'm almost embarrassed to state it.

I think most marriages die of neglect. Pure and simple neglect. Somewhere we were handed the idea that True Love, when it happens, will burst into flames by some spontaneous combustion, and that once you get married the fire will burn on its own. But, as I have argued in this book, love rarely happens spontaneously. Usually we create it. And when love is kept aflame, year after year, it is because two people do a great number of things to keep the fire replenished. Ignored, love very quickly sputters and dies. "The roots of the deepest love," someone once wrote, "die in the heart if not tenderly cherished." Dante put the same idea even more dramatically:

> We know for how brief a while
> In woman's heart the fire of love can burn
> If eye and hand 'plenish it not, afresh.[96]

It might seem obvious that if a love relationship is a complicated reciprocal system of meeting each other's needs, the system will require considerable work to keep it functioning smoothly. Yet we hear over and over that one should not have to "work at love." We are told that if two people "really love each other," they should be able to relax and be spontaneous. Just let it happen.

That sounds marvelous and carefree, but I don't know anything of value that doesn't require time, attention, and lots of maintenance.

I have owned homes for twenty-five years, and I'm still amazed at how much one must do to keep a house from falling down. The forces of nature—things like gravity and the sun—cause the house to revert to its natural state. It will crumble if you let it. Put off for a few months a one-hour repair job on the gutters, and you'll find yourself with a weekend of work to replace the rotted boards. The principle is that the longer you postpone maintenance, the faster the rate of deterioration.

I see that principle operating in families every day. Many couples who have come to my office with their marriages in shreds did not start fighting about unsolvable problems. Their marriages were not suffering from major malfunctions, but merely from a series of small deteriorations that a little adjusting and tightening could have corrected. But people had lost interest and had turned their attention to other things: children, careers, decorating their houses, tennis. The destruction had accelerated, and when they came to our offices, their houses were in shambles. Doors had fallen off their hinges, fuses had blown, circuits had overloaded, and the backup systems had rusted out.

My hunch is that we men are more inattentive than are women. Traditionally, at least, the male feels that success in his career is paramount. When this kind of man marries, he often breathes a great psychic sigh. Now he can focus all his energies on the great challenge of "making it" in what he sees as the "real world." He has, in effect, hired an assistant to take care of his private needs. This view of marriage as the base from which one is launched to higher things is an insidious enemy to lasting love relationships.

The corollary is that the best lover in the world may not be a good-looking or brilliant man, but he is a man who can focus 100 percent of his attention on the woman before him, and few women alive will not respond to that.

It is such intensity, as I have been saying, that ignites love in the first place. But then we obtusely assume that once ignited, the fire will burn by itself and we can turn our concentration to other things. But love must be refueled, nursed, nudged, blown on, and even shaken back to life. To see love as requiring such attention is not to cheapen or depreciate it. Quite to the contrary—we are saying that our love is important enough to watch it carefully, to tend its needs, to feed it with new fuel, and to keep it burning whatever the cost.

In 1957 Arlene Weiss was at a Manhattan party when a rum cake accidentally toppled off the refrigerator. Rather than see the hostess suffer hurt feelings, she and her new friend, a struggling young actor, sat down and ate the cake off the floor with spoons.

"We were the only two people who did it," she recalled recently, "and I think it cemented our friendship for life. That sort of playfulness has stood us in good stead for twenty-four years."

The struggling young actor was Alan Alda, and he and Arlene have now been married a quarter of a century. Naturally, their relationship has come under close scrutiny by the press. Everyone wants to know their secret. No, they have no formula, but Alda is willing to philosophize. "Love returns in waves," he says. "Waves of puppy love that feel more vibrant than the first blush of romance at twenty. That's followed by waves of utter discontent. Yes, utter detestation. You just have to wait it out."

According to interviewers, Arlene is not glamorous. She does her own hair, wears little makeup, and looks like many other middle-aged suburban housewives. How has she sustained her relationship with the millionaire superstar who is one of the most admired men in America? "Personal chemistry, more than anything else," she replies. "We both have a good sense of humor; we like to talk a lot; we play games . . . and we read to each other." It is obviously a friendship that encompasses, among other things, romance.

"The essence of living together, really," says Alda, "is heightening your awareness in very specific ways of what the people around you are doing. . . . See what the other people are wearing, know what your kid got in the last science test, notice if your kid wears the same clothes every day. . . . Arlene and I have always valued our marriage, so we've put a lot of energy into making it what it is."[97]

The "heightened awareness" that Alda is talking about is simply a matter of the will. It is not so much a talent as it is a decision. If when you talk to your mate you are half asleep and unenthusiastic, then when a friend calls about tomorrow's golf date and your voice has lilt and laughter in it, that contrast is not lost on your mate. "I'll tell you what I want," a distraught woman said as she moved to the edge of her chair, "I want to be as important to my husband as his clients. When he talks to me as we drive somewhere in the car, he's disengaged and condescending. It's the same tone of voice when he talks to the kids. But let someone else call, and he suddenly perks up and gets animated."

Of course, we all have the right to kick back and disengage when we're home. Home should be a refuge from having to be "on" with the outside world. But if home becomes a group of relationships from which we are in the habit of disengaging, we are headed for trouble.

Ed Goldfader owns and operates Tracers Company of America, Inc., a New York agency that specializes in finding lost persons. He says more wives than ever are running away, not because they have found new lovers, but because they are bored and feel that there must be more to life than playing handmaiden to unappreciative husbands. A clue as to why the women feel unappreciated lies in this bit of information Goldfader supplied recently: when a man comes to Tracers for help in finding his wife, the agency asks questions about his wife's personal history and personal appearance. Often he is unable to remember the color of her eyes![98]

The Significance of Time

Someone has said that the best measuring stick of a person's scale of values is the way in which that person divides his or her time. Never mind what they say is important to them, the real indicator is the way they spend their days. And the best lovers are not necessarily the most sentimental people, but they are always the ones who spend a lot of hours with their lovers. Again and again I talk to husbands who have worked overtime for years, thinking that their financial success was going to make their wives happy, when their wives would have much preferred to have less money to spend and their husbands home in the evening.

I know of a woman who had married the weekend she graduated from college, had her first baby nine months later, and was married to a rather stiff and formal workaholic for almost thirty years. Her whole life had been circumscribed by her family, and her husband had never had a lot of time for her. Then, to everyone's amazement, she left her husband for a carpenter ten years younger than her, who was restoring an old house down the street. He looked very much like a student in his beard and jeans, and I was perplexed by what attracted her and gave her the courage to buck tradition, the scorn of her children, and the disapproval of her friends. "He has time for me," she replied. "Of course it's flattering to have a younger man interested in you, but it's not that primarily. He wants to do all the silly things I've always wanted to do. He works thirty-five hours a week and that's all. We go to the zoo. We spend hours shopping and cooking exotic recipes and then sitting down to romantic candlelight dinners."

She may well find that she has made a mistake, but there is a lesson for us all in that situation. The greatest gifts we can give the person we love are large chunks of our time. It is a more cherished gift than any present in a box.

Nick Stinnett, who is chairman of the Human Development and Family Department at the University of Nebraska, decided to study strong families and determine what were their common strengths. Here are some of the important things he found in almost every solid family:

- *A high degree of religious orientation.* Not all belonged to an organized church, but nearly all considered themselves highly religious.
- *Appreciation.* Family members gave one another compliments and sincere psychic "strokes."
- *Time together.* In all areas of their lives, meals, work, recreation, the family members structured their schedules to spend time together.[99]

Many families grow apart not because they are poorly matched or because their purposes in life are in conflict; they grow apart simply because they do not take the time to build intimacy. As André Maurois has said, "Marriage is an edifice that must be rebuilt every day."[100]

My wife is an expert at the daily construction of such closeness. When I am taking my morning bath, she often comes in with her coffee cup in one hand, and a fresh cup for me in the other, and then she sits on the floor and talks about the day ahead of us. I regard it as a rather romantic moment, although she may not look all that glamorous in her curlers, and I'm *certainly* not very dashing there in the tub. But it's a moment of closeness because she carves out of her hectic morning some minutes to sit and talk to me.

Charlie and Martha Shedd are our good friends who have raised five children, survived more than forty years of marriage, and maintain a very tight love affair between each other still. From them, Diane and I got the concept of having regular spots of time with each other that are inviolate. After dinner, for instance, we get a few minutes to log in without children. In the summer, we stretch out on the reclining chairs in the back yard and see who can spot the first star. In the winters, we take our coffee into the living room and light a fire. The conversation is not always profound, and we are not necessarily whispering sweet nothings into each other's ears during that time; we're asking, "Who are you today, and how are you?" And the children seem to understand that those moments alone are important.

The second idea we have stolen from Charlie and Martha is the plan to have a meal out together each week. It's not when we're on our way to a play or a show, and it's not when we take out guests or the kids. It's usually Friday lunch. I see patients up until 12 or 1, then I knock off for the day. So we meet at some restaurant and have a leisurely two hours together, and then the rest of the afternoon is ours. Sometimes it's exciting, like walking through a museum or a park. Other times it's as humdrum as shopping at Sears. But we make sure we get to spend the afternoon together. Those Fridays are so important to me that if I'm away on a speaking trip, I do my best to fly in by noon on Friday.

Courtesy and Love

"Romance is just one cut beyond courtesy," some sage has noticed, and one of the clear demonstrations of love is that you continue to treat your mate with the same consideration that you did in the early stages of your romance. Love is kindness.

A group of Playboy bunnies were being interviewed on what they found attractive in a man. One talked about being on tour and a date who wanted to impress her in one city rented a helicopter at a cost of $900, which impressed her negatively. She was petrified of helicopters, and felt it was a ridiculous gesture. "It's the little things that count," she said, "not expensive dinners and champagne so much as a telephone call the next day, or his willingness to take my calls when he is in a meeting."

Rituals and gestures are terribly important in the sustaining of love, and the reason they count for so much is that they have a cumulative effect. If you are married to a person who has been thinking up little favors and small gestures of affection for years, that becomes a mortar that holds your relationship together when the crises come and rattle your marriage.

Skiing is my favorite avocation, and Snow Bird, Utah, is my favorite place to ski. When Diane and I had been married a year, the local snow was scarce, and money was even more scarce around our house. The living room was still bare of furniture, and I had resigned myself to a budget winter with no allocation for recreation, let alone a trip to an expensive place like Snow Bird.

On Christmas Day, Diane's last present for me was only a little envelope. But inside was a savings account passbook, in which were recorded little deposits she had been making secretly all year: $7.50 here, $5.00 there, squirreled away from her paycheck. Without my knowing, she had been saving all year to give me a ski trip for Christmas, and when she handed me the passbook, the account had added up to $1200.

So in January we left our furniture-free living room behind and had a glorious ten days in Utah. We ate shrimp until we couldn't walk, we skiied in the powdered snow, we drove to Salt Lake City to hear the Mormon Tabernacle Choir rehearse one cold night. We laughed and made love and absorbed together all the beauties there were to see in one week.

The furniture for the living room could come later, and

it did, but opportunities to witness each other's joy at a fresh snowstorm would never come again in just that fashion. During the week, I thought about all those months of Diane's planning for this—the lunches she'd skipped, the sales she'd passed up. Here was the thing that meant most: she had occupied many scattered moments during the year scheming and planning for something she knew would make me happy. One never forgets such acts of kindness; they help build up a friendship, like many layers of a fine lacquer finish.

It is the same with gifts: you can picture your lover walking through a department store, picking up sweaters, sorting through coats, thinking about you and remembering what you like and what you enjoy.

Being an artist at romance does not require so much a sentimental and emotional nature as it requires a thoughtful nature. When we think of the romantic things, we think of events that occur because someone made a choice to love. A man stops off at a florist and brings his wife a single rose in the evening, a girl makes her lover a lemon pie with just the degree of tartness he likes, a wife makes arrangements for her husband to take the caribou-hunting trip he thought he'd never afford—these are not the goo of sweet emotion, they are the stuff that comes from resolution and determination, and they are strong mortar.

Hanging on the wall here in the backyard shack where I sit at the typewriter is a cross fashioned from rough-sawn myrtle wood. It means a great deal to me not only because of the original act it symbolizes, but also because of the small act that brought it to me. Mark Svensson, my closest male friend for more than a decade, was not in the best of moods for a period of several months, and neither was I.

We still met every week for lunch, but for various reasons the conversation was stiff, and the friendship did not flow. I suspect that he, like me, wondered if our relationship, which had survived lots of blowups in the past, would endure this period of tension and uneasiness.

One day I came out to my shack and someone had hung a beautiful cross of myrtle, roughly and artistically sawn on a bandsaw and glued together. I knew immediately that Mark had dropped by earlier in the day, and not finding me at my desk, had leaned the cross against the wall. When I called he said, "Oh, I just had a few minutes before an appointment, and I wanted to make you something. I went out to the shop and that cross just seemed to happen as I fiddled with some wood at the bandsaw. Probably made it in twenty minutes, so don't think it's any big deal."

But to me it was a big deal. Even though things were lumpy between us, he had still wanted to show his affection with some gesture. And today, as I sit here working, that cross reminds me that if I'm to keep my relationships alive through the years, I must devote some time to the thoughtful gesture, the tender act, which sometimes shows more love than verbal protestation.

Companionate Love

Theodor Reik believes that it is possible for a passionate love to smooth out into something very fine:

A new kind of companionship, different from romance, but no less valuable, may result in a sense of ease and harmony. Although idealization has ceased and passion has gone, yet the atmosphere is clear and calm. The lover has changed into a friend. There is no longer the violence of love, but the peacefulness of tender attachment.[101]

Elaine Walster calls this type of love "companionate love":

> Most couples find, happily, that a friend is really what they needed all along.... Early in a relationship a couple needs something—passion—to bond them together, while they chip away at the rough spots that exist in any relationship. By the time passion flickers out, it has been replaced by companionate love—shared understandings, emotions, and habits. Passionate love is a fragile flower; it wilts in time. Companionate love is a sturdy evergreen; it thrives with contact.[102]

I may have a quibble with Walster about the inevitability of passionate love departing from a long-term relationship: I see couples who keep it coming back in recurring waves. But her and Reik's descriptions of companionate love are very attractive. How does one develop such a relationship? How does passionate love modulate into an affectionate friendship rather than an alienated disillusionment? It's not all that hard, according to Walster: you so arrange your shared life that you have a lot of happy hours together.

Here is an example of how someone like Alan Alda plans for such good hours to be shared. When he and Arlene celebrated their sixteenth wedding anniversary, they had some guests over, and one of them said he had to catch a midnight plane. Alan offered to drive him to the airport and asked Arlene to come along. At the gate Alan turned to her, pulled two plane tickets out of his pocket and said, "He isn't leaving, *we* are." And that was how Arlene found out Alan had secretly arranged a dream of hers: to go with him to Paris. He had taken care of her passport, rescheduled her appointments, packed her bags, and hired a sitter to stay with their daughters.[103] The affection expressed by such gestures will go a long way in creating a deep companionate love. The recollection of such acts becomes money in the bank. And in every good marriage there are occasions when you must draw on such reserves of kindness.

The great truths of the universe are always simple truths, and the great men and women are not afraid to utter the simple truths. When Nobel Prize winner Isaac Bashevis Singer was being interviewed about the qualities of a great writer, he cut through the reporter's attempts at false sophistication and said, "Two important things are to have a genuine interest in people and to be kind to them. Kindness, I've discovered, is everything in life."[104]

Young love is a flame—very pretty—often very hot and fierce, but still only light and flickering. The love of the older and disciplined heart is as coals, deep-burning, unquenchable.

—HENRY WARD BEECHER

It is love in old age, no longer blind, that is true love. For love's highest intensity doesn't necessarily mean its highest quality. Glamor and jealousy are gone; and the ardent caress, no longer needed, is valueless compared to the reassuring touch of a trembling hand. Passers-by commonly see little beauty in the embrace of young lovers on a park bench, but the understanding smile of an old wife to her husband is one of the loveliest things in the world.

—BOOTH TARKINGTON

Someone has written that love makes people believe in immortality, because there seems not to be room enough in life for so great a tenderness, and it is inconceivable that the most masterful of our emotions should have no more than the spare moments of a few years.

—ROBERT LOUIS STEVENSON

So faith, hope, love abide, these three; but the greatest of these is love.

—I CORINTHIANS 13:13

Epilogue

After writing most of the chapters of this book, I put the manuscript in my briefcase and caught a plane for Texas, to visit a couple who are living together. I wanted to see if the principles I have been elucidating in these pages would apply to their happy living arrangement.

These two are not youngsters and have been together for some time. Before deciding to move in with each other, they had given considerable thought to ways they could make theirs a mutually satisfying relationship. By now, he'd told me on the telephone, they'd worked out a lot of the bugs.

Their relationship is indeed unusual in some ways, but I must agree that it is working. They're rather quiet people by nature, but there is a strong, steady subterranean current

204 / The Romance Factor

of emotion between them. One day when he was at the store (he does most of the grocery shopping and much of the cleaning), she was standing at the sink washing vegetables while we talked. "Every month we live together," she said, "I'm more aware of what a terrific guy he is. He may be a man of few words, but he is very, very sensitive to my moods and my needs. He seems to notice what makes me happy, and I think he is the kindest man I've ever known." There was a long pause as she thought. "I don't think I've ever been happier," she said.

I came away convinced that these two had somewhere along the way eagerly and happily fallen in love, and they have found a way to live without being bothered, apparently, by the things that bother so many of us. She doesn't regard him as sexist or chauvinistic, like lots of feminists who have given up on male-female relationships. Sisterhood, however, is important to her. She is close to some women. In fact, she is much more gregarious than the man with whom she lives. She would probably like to have parties and dinners more often, but she doesn't want to rock his boat unduly, so instead she goes out to lunch with her cronies and comes home laughing, with fresh anecdotes. He is eager to hear the anecdotes, and that appears to be enough for her. She sees no conflict between her love for other women and this deep attachment to her man. And she has priorities: sisterhood may be great, but if she ever had to choose, it would be him. Hands down.

She would not make that choice because she feels dependent on him, surely, for she is probably more independent than he. They have the advantage of living in the country, on a farm, and perhaps they don't have to be looking out for Number One out of sheer self-defense, the way we city dwellers do. At any rate, neither of these two worry about the other encroaching on his or her turf.

I don't know what it is, exactly, that these two have between them. They have found some things they enjoy together and have built a kind of moat around these rituals. They like the same newscast each evening, and he regularly comes in from his work in time for that program. Not so much for the news, I suspect, as for the ritual of doing something together every day.

Rituals may have a lot to do with it. He never goes to the refrigerator for a soft drink without asking if she would like one. And I have watched her sit at the kitchen table for five minutes shaking a carafe of salad dressing to get it thoroughly mixed. She didn't say so, but I knew it was because he liked it that way.

It's remarkable, really, how their lives are intertwined. They've been together for some time now, so that he knows what type of squash she enjoys and will go to three stores if necessary to find it for her. She listens if he says he likes some dish, and she fixes it for him again soon. They know a great deal about each other's bodies and seem to know how to pleasure one other. They touch a lot. But never in public, and they even seemed a little bashful doing it around me. But obviously they have made it their business to learn what turns the other on sexually, and have managed to include lots of those things in their life together.

Perhaps their relationship works because it's an arrangement between equals, with each partner ready to give solace and share responsibility. In short, these two do not seem very self-centered. Although there is a healthy amount of self-starting independence in each, they are not forever taking their own emotional pulses. They appear to be more interested in taking the other's pulse, and doing things that bring the other pleasure.

I know that it is a medieval word, coming from the arena of religious life, but it is the only word I can think of to describe them: they have a certain *devotion* to each other. Neither was coerced into it, and I suppose that either could decide to leave this life of service any time he or she wanted, but yes, it is a little similar to the vows one takes to enter a religious order. You give up some things to enter the service of God. In fact, now that I think of it, this is part of what the social scientists find objectionable about the idealized view of romance—it has much of the trappings of the twelfth-century troubadour, who pledged himself in devotion and service to his lady.

The couple I visited probably would have been embarrassed if I compared their living arrangement to the fealty of knights and ladies, and they don't talk much about whether they're "in love," but their relationship has many of the signs. It's a delicate balance to maintain, but when such devotion works, it works wonderfully, like the ecstasy that Dante wrote of when he praised Beatrice in particular and Love in general. But then Dante was clearly in love with love.

There is a certain warmth in this couple's home that is rare in our day, when the rule is caution in relationships. I might go so far as to say that these two people have decided, deep in some inner chamber of themselves, to cherish each other. If she made some such decision, I'm certain that she knew—because she's a woman of intelligence—that she was taking a large risk, allowing herself to be vulnerable that way. Nevertheless, something must have clicked inside her, and the lucky thing in this case is that he heard the click, and something similar happened to him. But maybe it wasn't all luck. Maybe there was some spontaneous generation of emotion, a chemistry that occurred between them, as in a breeder reactor. Love is that way. It breeds more love.

That's my hunch, but I don't know, because I didn't ask.

They are that kind of people—you see it between them, but you don't want to pry, or ask them to talk too much about what they have. It is like a delicate sunset: not to be discussed so much as admired.

They *did* discuss with me the celebration they held when they moved in together. They had agreed by then that there was something between them that neither wanted to lose, so they asked a couple of friends to come over for a little party, where they would explain about their new living arrangement. Others heard about it and wanted to come, and it turned out to be quite a crowd.

These two must have been a little frightened to talk about their love. It's one thing to commit yourself to a life of devotion, quite another to announce it to your friends. Lots of people make idealistic resolutions that they're not sure they can live up to, so they hedge their bets and don't tell anyone. But these two went public with their love, and I think that helped to cement it.

I wish I could have been there to hear what they said at that party, but I couldn't attend. Some of the people were probably turned off by the sentimental nature of their talk. They indicated their desire to love each other even if one became handicapped or ill, and even used words like "honor" and "devotion."

The other thing that was surprising, in this age of impermanence, was their statement that this was not to be a temporary arrangement. They said that they wanted to try to stay together. There was no nonsense about exclusivity of sexual attraction—they knew they'd be attracted to others at times, but they made a pact not to chase every sexual impulse like the rabbits out in their hutches. Instead they would be true to each other. They even used that word—*true.*

Of course they took a gamble to say all that, and it will

be embarrassing to face their friends when and if they split up. If it doesn't work they'll get ribbed about all that romantic idealism.

Since there was such a crowd, and because they are highly religious people, my friends had their party at a nearby church, and asked the minister to attend. There was, I understand, one cynic present who said he'd read that such relationships based on romance usually end in about eighteen months. And who knows? It may not last forever.

But so far so good. Those two happen to be my parents, and it's been some time since they made those promises to each other. This June they celebrated their fiftieth wedding anniversary.

Notes

1. Erich Fromm, *To Have Or To Be?* (New York: Harper & Row, 1976), p. 45.
2. William Lederer, *Marital Choices* (New York: Norton, 1981), p. 48.
3. Jessie Kornbluth, "Love Stories," *Redbook,* January 1977, p. 16.
4. Dorothy Tennov, *Love and Limerence* (New York: Stein and Day, 1979); Denis de Rougemont, *Love in the Western World,* trans. Montgomery Belgion, rev. ed. (New York: Pantheon, 1956). De Rougemont can even pinpoint the beginnings of romance with a date! He tells us that it began with a letter between Héloïse and Abelard in 1118 (pp. 74-75). De Rougemont has a legitimate point to make, but like many evangelists, he gets carried away with his thesis and seriously overstates the case.
5. Genesis 29:20.
6. Song of Solomon 7:6-8.
7. Betty Miller, *Robert Browning* (New York: Scribner's, 1952), p. 76.
8. Elizabeth Barrett Browning, *Sonnets from the Portuguese* (New York: Grosset & Dunlap, 1974), p. 89.
9. Erich Fromm, *The Art of Loving* (New York: Harper & Row, Perennial Library, 1956), p. 4.

10. Dorothy Tennov, *Love and Limerence* (New York: Stein and Day, 1979), p. 145.

11. Diogenes Laertius, *Aristotle*, bk. V, sec. 19.

12. Plutarch, *Conjugal Precepts.*

13. John Money, *Love and Love Sickness* (Baltimore: Johns Hopkins University Press, 1980), p. 65.

14. Ernest Becker, *Angel in Armor* (New York: Free Press, 1969), pp. 14–15.

15. *People,* January 19, 1981, p. 78.

16. Judith Viorst, "To Be or Not To Be . . . Beautiful," *Redbook,* August 1976, p. 190.

17. Elaine Walster and G. William Walster, *A New Look at Love* (Reading, Mass.: Addison-Wesley, 1978), p. 55.

18. George Harris, Introduction, in Walster and Walster, *A New Look at Love,* p. vii.

19. Anäis Nin, *The Diaries of Anäis Nin,* ed. Gunther Stuhlmann, vol. 5 (New York: Harcourt Brace Jovanovich, 1974), p. 34.

20. Marion Zola, *All the Good Ones Are Married* (New York: Times Books, 1981), pp. 39–40.

21. Robert J. Levin, Virginia E. Johnson, and William H. Masters, *The Pleasure Bond* (New York: Bantam, 1976), p. 253.

22. Psalm 34:5.

23. Galatians 5:22–23.

24. James Bender, "Be Glad You're Not Beautiful," *Reader's Digest,* October 1950, p. 84.

25. Susan Sadd and Carol Tavris, *The Redbook Report on Female Sexuality* (New York: Delacorte, 1977), pp. 97–106. Such volunteer surveys have some notorious failings, of course, and do not represent a cross section of the population so much as a particular type of reader of a particular magazine. A *Good Housekeeping* poll at about the same time, for instance, revealed that only about half as many of their readers had engaged in premarital sex as had *Redbook* readers. Sexually nervous readers of either magazine would not be expected to fill out a questionnaire on such a topic. But of the 100,000 women who *did* respond, the religious readers reported clearly more satisfying sex lives.

26. Albert E. Kahn, *Joys and Sorrows* (New York: Simon & Schuster, 1970), p. 17.

27. Harriet Van Horne, "Romance vs. Sex Appeal: The Battle Women Lost," *Glamour,* November 1961, p. 103.

28. E. J. Kanin, K. D. Davidson, and S. R. Scheck, "A Research Note on Male-Female Differentials in the Experience of Heterosexual Love," *Journal of Sex Research,* 1970, *6,* 64–72.

29. Elaine Walster and G. William Walster, *A New Look at Love* (Reading, Mass.: Addison-Wesley, 1978), p. 50.

30. W. Waller, *The Family: A Dynamic Interpretation* (New York: Dryden, 1938), p. 243.

31. Anthony Pietropinto and Jacqueline Simenauer, *Beyond the Male Myth* (New York: Times Books, 1977), p. 208.

32. Susan Sadd and Carol Tavris, *The Redbook Report on Female Sexuality* (New York: Delacorte, 1977), pp. 131–132.

33. Judith Viorst, "What Is This Thing Called Love?" *Redbook,* February 1975, pp. 15–16.

34. Hazel Andre, "My Last Wonderful Days," *Farm Journal,* July 1956, pp. 31–32, 86.

35. Abraham Maslow, *Religions, Values, and Peak-Experiences* (New York: Penguin, 1976), pp. 86–87.

36. Marghanita Laski, *Ecstasy: A Study of Some Secular and Religious Experiences* (New York: Greenwood Press, 1968), pp. 187–206. Laski also lists antitriggers, such as the presence of crowds, commercialism, litter, the exercise of reason, brutality, war, ugliness.

37. Ibid., pp. 116–121.

38. Erich Fromm, *The Art of Loving* (New York: Harper & Row, Perennial Library, 1956), p. 44.

39. It is normal, of course, for the frequency of coitus to level out when a couple have been together for some time. According to Norman Lobsenz, the average rate of intercourse drops from three times a week for couples in their twenties to once a week for those in their forties. But that statistic probably reveals more about the familiarity of the couples with each other than their age. In one survey of women, for instance, twenty-five percent of the newly married wives said they had sex more than four times a week. That proportion dropped to twelve percent of the women married over a year, seven percent of those married over five years, and five percent of those married eight years or longer. (Norman Lobsenz, "Seven Ways to Bring Sex Back to Life," *Reader's Digest,* March 1981, p. 35; *Redbook Report,* p. 67.)

40. Marabel Morgan, *Total Woman* (Old Tappan, N.J.: Revell, 1973), pp. 117–118.

41. Interview October 11, 1979, by Kathleen Newton, University of Southern California News Service, Los Angeles, California.

42. Susan Sadd and Carol Tavris, *The Redbook Report Report on Female Sexuality* (New York: Delacorte, 1977), p. 68.

43. Albert Goldman, *Elvis* (New York: McGraw-Hill, 1981).

44. Philip G. Zimbardo, *Shyness* (New York: Harcourt Brace Jovanovich, 1978), p. 25.

45. *Los Angeles Times,* November 5, 1981, p. 22.

46. *Love and Marriage* (New York: Berkley, 1981), p. 80.

47. Anders Nygren, *Agape and Eros,* trans. A. G. Herbert (New York: Macmillan, 1932), 3 vols. For a more balanced Christian view of eros, see M. C. D'Arcy, *The Mind and Heart of Love* (New York: Holt, 1947).

48. Dwight Small, *How Should I Love You?* (San Francisco: Harper & Row, 1979), p. 158.

49. Lewis B. Smedes, *Love Within Limits* (Grand Rapids, Mich.: Eerdmans, 1978), p. 129.

50. C. S. Lewis, *The Four Loves* (New York: Harcourt Brack Jovanovich, 1960). Curiously enough, Lewis and Freud agree at this juncture. Although Freud was more relaxed about simple sex, he saw romantic love as pathological, and for the same reason. He regarded it as "regression to a state of limitless narcissism." *Civilization and It's Discontents,* trans. J. Riviere (London: Hogarth Press, 1953), p. 21.

51. Matthew 22:39.

52. Anders Nygren, *Agape and Eros,* trans. A. G. Herbert (New York: Macmillan, 1932), 3 vols., vol. I, p. 170.

53. Erik Erickson, *Childhood and Society,* 2nd ed. (New York: Norton, 1963), pp. 263–264.

54. Nicholas Johnson, "Test Pattern for Living," *Saturday Review,* May 29, 1971, p. 33.

55. William Kilpatrick, *Identity & Intimacy* (New York: Delacorte, 1975), p. 24. I am indebted to Kilpatrick for calling my attention to authors quoted in this chapter as well as in succeeding sections.

56. Robert Bolt, *A Man for All Seasons* (New York: Random House, 1962), p. 140.

57. Ibid., p. xii.

58. Alice Rossi, "Transition to Parenthood," *Journal of Marriage and the Family,* 1968, *30* (1), 34.

59. Genevieve Knupfer, Walter Clark, and Robin Room, "The Mental Health of the Unmarried," *American Journal of Psychiatry,* 1966, *122,* 847.

60. Quoted in F. W. Dillistone, "Revival or Removal?" *Theology Today,* October 1953, p. 299.

61. Kahil Gibran, *The Prophet* (New York: Knopf, 1923), p. 15.

62. Alan Loy McGinnis, *The Friendship Factor* (Minneapolis: Augsburg, 1979), pp. 76–78.

63. *Los Angeles Times,* November 11, 1981, part V, p. 1.

64. Will and Ariel Durant, *A Dual Autobiography* (New York: Simon & Schuster, 1977), p. 50.

65. Arthur Sueltz, *Life at Close Quarters* (Waco, Tex.: Word Publishing, in press).

66. Frederick S. Perls, *Gestalt Therapy Verbatim*, ed. John O. Stevens (Lafayette, Calif., Real People Press, 1969), p. 4.

67. Victor Frankl, *Psychotherapy and Existentialism* (New York: Simon & Schuster, 1968), p. 104.

68. Matthew 22: 37–39.

69. This case adapted from James McCary, *Freedom and Growth in Marriage* (New York: Hamilton, 1975), pp. 115–117.

70. Reported by Marian Christ, *Reader's Digest*, December 1974, p. 201.

71. Alan Paton, "The Challenge of Fear," *Saturday Review*, September 9, 1967, p. 20.

72. Jessie Bernard, *The Future of Marriage* (New York: Bantam, 1973), p. 63; Angus Campbell, "The American Way of Mating: Marriage Sí, Children Only Maybe," *Psychology Today*, May 1975, p. 37; William J. Lederer and Don D. Jackson, *The Mirages of Marriage* (New York: Norton, 1968), pp. 69–74.

73. *Ladies Home Journal*, July 1980, pp. 91, 146. All this must be taken with a grain of salt, because many of the childless couples who were unhappy with each other are already divorced by the time of such surveys. Nevertheless, it is quite clear from that data that the presence of children impedes romance rather than enhances it.

74. *Los Angeles Times*, April 15, 1981, part V, p. 2.

75. Bruce Larson, *No Longer Strangers* (Waco, Texas: Word Publishing, 1971), pp. 104–105.

76. Related by Mrs. Allen T. Edmunds, *Reader's Digest*, January 1982, p. 85.

77. Robert Fontaine, "My Mother's Hands," *Atlantic Monthly*, March 1957, pp. 65–67.

78. Ivor Davis, "Paul and Joanne," *Extra*, December 1980, p. 88.

79. Pietropinto and Simenauer, pp. 278–281; Elin Schoen, "Can You Love More Than One?" *Redbook*, July 1976, pp. 83ff. It is clear from these surveys that there is a correlation between women working and the amount of their extramarital activity. They report that 47 of 100 working wives have had affairs, as opposed to 27 of 100 housebound wives. But it is not easy to determine what is cause and what is effect.

80. Ronald Mazur, *The New Intimacy* (Boston: Beacon, 1973), p. 12.

81. Elin Schoen, "Can You Love More Than One?" *Redbook*, July 1976, p. 163.

82. Avodah Offit, *Night Thoughts: Reflections of a Sex Therapist* (New York: Congdon and Lattes, 1981), pp. 43–49.

83. Denis de Rougemont, *Love in the Western World*, trans. Montgomery Belgion, rev. ed. (New York, Pantheon, 1956).

84. Nora Scott Kinzer, "Soapy Sin in the Afternoon," *Psychology Today*, August 1973, p. 46.

85. Richard DeVoss, *Believe* (Old Tappan, N.J.: Revell, 1975), p. 101.

86. David Reuben, "Why Wives Cheat on their Husbands," *Reader's Digest*, August 1973, p. 124.

87. Ibid.

88. Phillip Lopate, *Bachelorhood: Tales of the Metropolis* (Boston: Little, Brown, 1981), p. 36.

89. Andrew Greeley, *Thy Brother's Wife* (New York: Warner, 1982), p. 351.

90. Mary Ann Bartusis. *Every Other Man* (New York; Dutton, 1978), pp. xii–xiii.

91. Søren Kierkegaard, *The Works of Love,* in Robert Bretall, ed., *A Kierkegaard Anthology* (New York: Modern Library, 1946), p. 293.

92. Dale Carnegie, *How to Win Friends and Influence People* (New York: Pocket Books, 1940), p. 235; Richard W. Davis, *Disraeli* (Boston: Little, Brown, 1976); André Maurois, *Disraeli,* trans. Hamish Miles (New York: Appleton, 1928).

93. C. S. Lewis, *Mere Christianity,* Macmillan Paperbacks ed. (New York: Macmillan, 1960), p. 116.

94. Carl Rogers, *Becoming Partners: Marraige and Its Alternatives* (New York: Delacorte, 1972), p. 25.

95. Harry S. Truman, *Memoirs of Harry S. Truman,* vol. 1 (Garden City, N.Y.: Doubleday, 1955), p. 116.

96. Quoted in T. H. Van deVelde, *Ideal Marriage* (New York: Covies Friede, 1926), p. 142.

97. Elizabeth Kaye, "Arlene and Alan Alda: A Love Story," *McCall's,* January 1976, p. 122.

98. Gail Sheehy, *Passages* (New York: Dutton, 1976), p. 264.

99. Nick Stinnett, "In Search of Strong Families," in Barbara Chesser, John DeFrain, and Nick Stinnett, eds., *Building Family Strengths* (Lincoln: University of Nebraska Press, 1979), pp. 23–37.

100. Quoted in Norman M. Lobsenz, "Building on the Positives in Marriage," *Reader's Digest,* April 1972, p. 172.

101. Theodor Reik, *A Psychologist Looks at Love* (New York: Holt, Rinehart, & Winston, 1972), p. 150.

102. Elaine Walster and G. William Walster, *A New Look at Love* (Reading, Mass.: Addison-Wesley, 1978), p. 125.

103. Elizabeth Kaye, "Arlene and Alan Alda: A Love Story," *McCall's,* January 1976, p. 16.

104. *Christian Science Monitor,* September 5, 1978, p. 28.